Shattered Souls Made Whole

Call anytime
336-944-5751

Shattered Souls Made *Whole*

Healing Heartache from Separation or Divorce

Valerie Sullivan

XULON PRESS ELITE

Xulon Press Elite
2301 Lucien Way #415
Maitland, FL 32751
407.339.4217
www.xulonpress.com

Xulon Elite

© 2019 by Valerie J Sullivan

All rights reserved solely by the author. The author guarantees all contents are original and do not infringe upon the legal rights of any other person or work. No part of this book may be reproduced in any form without the permission of the author. The views expressed in this book are not necessarily those of the publisher.

Scripture quotations taken from the King James Version (KJV) – *public domain*.

Printed in the United States of America.

ISBN-13: 9781545670125

Dedication

This book is dedicated to my children:
Brandon, Kyle, Catherine, Jasper, Kathryn, Joshua, and Kandis
I am proud to be your mom and wish with all my heart God's blessings will fall on you in abundance. I love you so very much!

My hope for all of you, as stated by the Apostle John, is this, *"Beloved, I wish above all things that thou mayest prosper and be in health, even as thy soul prospereth" (3 John 1:2).*

Table of Contents

Dedication v
Introduction ix
Lesson 1: Soul Wounds 1
Lesson 2: Our Secret Weapon 34
Lesson 3: Dealing with a Liar 73
Lesson 4: Putting it All Together 114
Lesson 5: Moving the Heart of God 147
Lesson 6: Handling Regrets and Dealing with Depression . . 180
Lesson 7: Overcoming Rejection, Bitterness, and
    Forgiveness 213
Lesson 8: Finding Your Purpose 241
Words of Gratitude 272
Works Cited 277

Introduction

*I*f you are separated or divorced, you may feel like the walking wounded.

I once was one of the walking wounded going through a painful separation. I knew I needed help to move through the process in a healthy way, whether that process led to a divorce or what I ultimately wanted which was reconciliation.

I went to my local Christian book store to find a book on separation and healing. I looked for something that would give me encouragement and tell me my situation would get better and would show me how to manage in the meantime. I desperately wanted to read a book that would tell me how to heal from this pain, so I could function, while still keeping any hope of reconciliation alive.

I couldn't find a single book to match my needs.

After walking out of the book store empty-handed, I told God that *He* was going to have to show me how to be healed because there was no text book, manuscript, or road map to show me. I cried out to God for help, and thankfully, He answered my prayers. He showed me step by step how to be completely healed.

This book is a product of those lessons. It is not so much my story, although I reference some of my individual challenges, as it is a step-by-step process of understanding biblical truths that will put you on the same path to healing.

Before I even asked God to teach me, He was beginning His work in me through my own journals. I would start an entry by pouring out my pain and anguish to God. By the end, I was turning to Him. I saw the pattern almost daily. The model I saw in my personal journals was the same one I saw as I was reading the book of Psalms. King David had the same habit of pouring out his broken heart to God, but then coming around to the realization that God was there guiding and comforting Him.

When my husband left and the bottom dropped out of my world, I was in shock. I felt confused, betrayed, broken-hearted, and shattered. It was as if a death had occurred, but he was still alive. My mind was unable to comprehend this new reality, and I found myself unable to eat, sleep, or think clearly. Some people are able to go to work, tuck those emotions away, and fake it until they get home. Unfortunately, I am not one of those people. I'm a "let it all hang out" kind of person. Because of this, it gave many well-intentioned people the opportunity to give me unwanted advice, such as, "There is someone better out there for you," "God has a plan," and

Introduction

"Time heals all wounds." Those remarks used to make me angry and frustrated. Maybe you can relate.

You will not hear me using cliché phrases, and I don't have a magic wand. A verse in Proverbs 25:20 resonates with me and maybe it will with you too. It can be paraphrased this way: Don't sing songs to a heavy heart. When I was in such pain, I did not want to hear platitudes, so that is not what I will offer you.

But what I can offer is knowledge of how the healing process begins and ends through uncovering and utilizing tools from the Bible. That way, you will be equipped to start the healing process on your own, in your own time, and you can follow the individual path God wants you to take. This healing and life-changing experience begins at the feet of the Great Physician, the Balm of Gilead, and the One who can heal you from all your soul wounds.

Throughout the book I include snippets of my journals and King David's journal, the book of Psalms. I hope you will find encouragement knowing that others have gone through similar hurts and heartaches and have learned to journey through and beyond. We can pray, as King David did in Psalm 4:4, *"...LORD, be merciful unto me: heal my soul."*

WARNING: This book is going to be more than your typical self-help book. It will be raw, real, challenging, and—if you apply the principles—life-changing. I encourage you to find a time where you can relax, uninterrupted if possible, to read the eight lessons

God gave me for healing. Each lesson builds on the previous, so reading Chapters 1-4 in order is highly recommended. The other chapters can be delved into as needed.

Be assured this book is in your hands for a reason.

Pray for God's protection over you and your family throughout each day. And remember, without a fight, there is never a victory! Don't get discouraged if you feel like you're taking two steps forward and one step back. Keep moving forward, and God will take you to a place of healing.

God bless you, and I pray that you will find healing for your soul as you journey through this book.

Lesson 1

Soul Wounds: What are they and how do we get them?

Separation and divorce bring a world of hurt. In this book I'll be sharing my story of separation and divorce and the lessons God taught me. Even though your particular situation may differ from mine, I believe you'll be able to relate to my experiences, feelings, and thoughts. Mostly, I hope you'll be drawn to the Lord, the way I was knowing He is our Hope as we navigate our struggles during separation. I know many reading this book will be hoping and praying for reconciliation, and for some that will come about. Others will have a marriage that ultimately leads to divorce. Either way, those broken relationships inevitably cause deep wounds. Wherever you find yourself, there is no judgement, just prayers for a God-given healing to envelope your heart.

On November 20, 2015, my life took a sharp turn that I could have never anticipated. From that moment throughout the next year, God gave me eight specific lessons on how to deal with a broken relationship. As I walked through the lessons and applied what I learned, I found that feelings of low self-confidence, fear, rejection, abandonment, anger, and bitterness were slowly replaced with trust, security, peace, love, and forgiveness. I also found a confidence that *"I can do all things through Christ who strengthens me"* (Philippians 4:13).

I believe the same thing will happen to you as you read and apply the Scriptures in this book. The lessons God taught me were powerful and life-changing. I know the same regeneration of life can be yours to experience as well.

When my husband said he "needed a break from the children and me" and left the house, my whole world turned upside down. At that moment, nothing could have prepared me for the set of circumstances in which I found myself. His announcement was sudden with little to no warning, and he was determined to follow this course of action with little discussion. It was not what I anticipated in my life.

Let me give you a little background. I grew up in a pastor's home and went to a Christian school from sixth grade through my senior year. I was taught about God, faith, and all the moral codes that went along with living the Christian life. I lived and loved

Soul Wounds: What Are They And How Do We Get Them?

those biblical values and beliefs, and passed them along to my children through devotions, homeschooling, and church attendance.

Now, everything I had known and believed was in question. I questioned God, whom my husband and I had served together. I questioned the Bible that gave us direction on how to live our lives. Everything I had placed my faith in was being examined: the Bible, God, my value system, and my husband. I had so many questions. Who was this man I had fiercely loved for the past nine years? Wasn't God the One who put the two of us together? My husband was Prince Charming, the dashing hero who came in, treated me like a princess, and gave me a fairy tale ending. Why would a God who loved me take that away? Why would a man who proclaimed to love God so intently throw it all away? So began my journey of making decisions to believe or not to believe, to stand in faith in God and the Bible, or to throw my beliefs away.

In the early days of our separation, I tumbled into a pit of despair and hurt. I hoped tomorrow would be better than today. I hoped God would turn this awful wrong into a right, somehow, someway.

I wrote this in my journal:

---❋---

November 26, 2015
"It's been six days since my husband, my soulmate, my best friend left me. I have fallen into a deep depression and can't seem to keep myself from spiraling down further. My goal is just to survive, to just get through the next hour or even the next five minutes. I was told I suffered a 'death' and will go through all the grieving

stages: shock, disbelief, denial, anger, guilt, bitterness, and resignation. I almost think actual, physical death would be preferable to this sudden separation. This vague, unknown, completely unexpected, bewildering, out-of-character event has left me stunned, breathless in shock and horror. God, what is happening? I have to figure this out."

As time went on, I wanted the hurts and painful moments to birth something new and amazing. I wanted a wonderful, beautiful ending to this story; with the proverbial silver lining and all, whatever my all-knowing God thought would be best. My vision was that Walt Disney happy ending. Of course, being in my mid-40s, the flawless, beautiful complexion and body of the princess and handsome prince with a true six-pack might be a bit of a stretch; hence I adjusted my fantasy ending slightly. I supposed it would be okay if both of us have some "character," a term my family affectionately uses whenever someone or something is not perfect.

"God," I prayed, "how am I supposed to be healed from the damage done by two people being torn in two? You said in Your Word that when we spoke our wedding vows, we 'became one flesh,' but now we are broken and bleeding from being ripped apart. I do not understand any of this. My husband and I had enjoyed one another and had so much in common. We taught Sunday school, sang together at church each Sunday, and taught Your Word to others. He preached behind the pulpit, and we both grew up with pastors as fathers. We actually had fun together. What more could

Soul Wounds: What Are They And How Do We Get Them?

a husband or wife want? How did this happen, and how do I deal with it? I am terribly wounded from the lies, betrayal, abandonment, and feelings of rejection."

During separation I experienced so many emotions: anger, confusion, bitterness, hopelessness, grief, sadness, and more. I'm sure you have, too. I knew I needed to move beyond these feelings to experience healing. I wasn't sure how to do that, but as I began to pray with desperation, seek God out, and study His Word, I began to discover the healing process.

Sources other than God, such as friends and family, will definitely provide needed support and comfort during the separation or divorce, but ultimately the truth we need for healing can be found in God and His Word.

The starting place for healing is to understand soul wounds. Your response might be to think, *Of course, I understand my wounds. They're from this person who is causing more pain than I could imagine.* That's an understandable response. And God wants us to pour out our hearts to Him. But He also wants us to find healing, and that means moving beyond this response.

Just as a doctor cannot prescribe the correct medicine without getting a proper diagnosis, we cannot understand how healing can take place if we don't grasp we are wounded, where that wound resides, and how to accomplish the feat of total healing.

I know it might be difficult to look at these wounds. It was for me. But I knew deep down I had to do this. Will you prayerfully consider doing the same?

One more thing. The healing process is not linear; this is not a step-by-step guide. You may move forward and then back, and then forward again. That's okay.

Intimate prayers, like the one below, can be very helpful.

Lord,

Will You give me willingness and courage to look at the wounds from this separation? You have seen my tears, and You know my pain. I want to move past this, but many days I don't know if that's even possible. Please open my eyes to Your truth and Your pathway to healing.

Amen

Let's get started looking at the healing process.

The healing process begins with

1) Understanding and acknowledging our soul wounds.

2) Taking action to heal from these soul wounds.

Our DNA

Before we head into specifically understanding how to heal from soul wounds, let's first take a look at our make-up—how God made us. God says we are made in the image of God (Genesis

Soul Wounds: What Are They And How Do We Get Them?

1:27). Just as God is made up of three parts—God the Father, God the Son, and God the Holy Spirit—we too are made up of three parts. We know that we are made up of body, soul, and spirit, as the apostle Paul references in 1 Thessalonians 5:23, *"And the very God of peace sanctify you wholly; and I pray God your whole **spirit** and **soul** and **body** be preserved blameless unto the coming of our Lord Jesus Christ."*

The body is the physical form that houses the soul and the spirit.

Our spirit is the spiritual side of us that is either made alive through salvation in Jesus Christ or dead without Jesus Christ. When we ask Jesus Christ to be our Savior, our spirit is instantly made perfect through the Holy Spirit.

The soul is made up of our mind, our will, and our emotions; in essence, it comprises who we are as individuals.

When we go through a separation or divorce, our souls are wounded and need healing. God taught me everyone receives soul wounds, and He taught me specifically how to deal with the soul wounds inflicted from broken relationships. He helped me understand what those wounds really are, where they come from, and how they can be remedied.

In Psalm 41:4 we see that David asks for his soul to be healed: *"I said, Lord, be merciful unto me: heal my soul..."*

If his soul needed to be healed, then we can properly surmise he had hurts, pain, wounds, and/or trauma of some kind that needed to be healed. This is where the idea of a soul wound comes into the picture.

Soul Wounds Defined

You might be wondering, "What exactly is a soul wound, and why should I care?" As we go through this chapter, you will clearly understand soul wounds and why being healed properly from those wounds matters.

One motivating factor is found in III John 1:2

"Beloved, I wish above all things that thou prosper and be in health, even as thy soul prospereth."

So what exactly is a soul wound?

My personal definition of a soul wound is an internal wound that causes a person to feel a negative emotion, such as hurt, bitterness, anger, rage, etc., that festers as time goes on.

Soul Wounds: What Are They And How Do We Get Them?

Soul wounds are generally initiated by hurt, traumas, or betrayal inflicted upon us by others or through our own sin. When someone mistreats us, we are wounded. Each time we sin, we are wounded. Some soul wounds are small, like papercuts; others are large gashes of great severity. For example, if someone forgets our birthday, we might be slightly wounded. If a friend or co-worker backstabs us or offends us by being two-faced, that might be a small tear. If we lie to our spouse or child or steal from the office, the laceration on our soul might be a little larger.

Huge, gaping soul wounds occur in cases such as adultery, rape, separation, divorce, or witnessing a murder or death.

Take for example a woman who is beaten by her husband, either physically or verbally. When a man stands and pledges his undying love, he also pledges to protect his wife. That is a vow he has given. When he uses his mouth or his fist to beat down his wife that pledge is broken, that trust is now gone, and painful wounds have been inflicted.

On the flip side, when a woman stands and pledges her undying love until "death do us part" but then chooses to reject her husband and sleep with another man, she breaks her vow. The trust is now gone, and painful wounds have been inflicted.

Now that I've defined soul wounds and given a couple of examples, let's dig deeper into why they matter.

We Are All Wounded

As life goes on year after year, we receive soul wounds from others or ourselves, beginning right from childhood. It is an inevitable part of life because we are fleshly beings prone to injuring ourselves and others. For example, have you ever been bullied, insulted, or even physically assaulted? If this happened to you as a child, it's likely left you with emotional soul wounds. As you age, in each phase of your life, you receive more wounds, possibly from parents, friends, a spouse, children, co-workers, pastors, or church people. If you really think about it, many people have inflicted pain on you, whether purposeful or not, even people you love and care about.

On the flipside, you have also imposed hurt upon others. Many times, those hurts were unintentional, but occasionally they were premeditated. When you remember these events and ponder these incidents even now, they probably still hurt or bring you some degree of remorse or humiliation. Along the way, we all try to deal with these wounds, but this does not always happen in a healthy way. Let's break down a couple possible real-life scenarios.

Let's say a husband is verbally abusive—it leaves a cut. The wife retreats, refusing to be intimate. Her husband becomes distant—a wound of rejection is born. And the cycle of reaction against the painful wounds begins with seemingly no end in sight and no ready remedy available to stop the cycle. Each can point a finger at the other person. Kind of like the chicken and the egg—which came first—who hurt who first and so the finger pointing begins.

Another scenario: A wife prepares a special romantic dinner at home with the candles lit and romantic moments planned for the night. The phone rings—the husband answers the work call and launches into a lengthy conversation. By the time the call is done the mood has been wrecked. She can see his mind is no longer on her but on the problems at the office. The wife is angered and verbally lashes out. The husband retreats—the cycle begins, more wounds inflicted.

Most likely, we don't even realize we are handling situations inappropriately. We feel justified in lashing out or retreating. In my case, I can say with certainty that I did not realize many of my unhealthy patterns. Can you remember a time when you handled a situation improperly and wounds occurred?

Acknowledging Soul Wounds

The first step towards understanding how to be deeply healed in our souls is to understand our own personal wounds. How do they come about? How do we attempt to deal with them in an unhealthy way? How can we uncover the pain and hurt so each wound can be identified and dealt with?

Each of us covers our injuries differently. Most of us handle our soul wounds in an unhealthy way by trying to divert attention from them, deny them, or cover them up when these occur in our youth. Some learn to be the class clown, while others shut down and retreat into themselves. Others push themselves to be the best at sports or academics or go to great lengths in seeking popularity. As we get older and continue trying to deal with these wounds, bad habits and diversions might form. Attempts to soothe those wounds might look like overeating, excessive shopping, obsessions, absorption with extracurricular activities, overachieving at work or sports, or constantly being driven to go, go, go. We also can become cynical, judgmental, harsh, or develop a mask and build walls that push people away in an effort not to get hurt again.

These coping mechanisms really do little more than create mind chatter to keep us distracted from the pain and from seeking a real solution.

Once we understand that we have soul wounds and we identify what they are, the next step is to make a choice about how to handle them: will we continue to try to cover them up, or will we deal with them by bringing them to God?

Healing is a Choice

I have always loved horses. I was blessed to spend my sixth-grade summer at my cousins' house. They had three beautiful

Soul Wounds: What Are They And How Do We Get Them?

horses and three Shetland ponies. I remember a particular time when one horse rubbed against barbed wire and received a gash on its rump. It was a pretty deep gash, about six inches long. The wound bled a little, and as the wound scabbed over you could see dried blood all around it. Gnats and flies buzzed around the wound and settled on the sore which was a disgusting, germy mess that even a ten-year-old kid thought was gross. The injured horse whipped its tail up every now and again to shoo the flies away, but they quickly returned. My uncle eventually saw it, gently led the horse to the barn, cleaned the injury, and applied ointment, a special salve that would protect it from the flies, seal the wound, and aid in the healing.

Just as gnats and flies were attracted to the seeping wound of that horse, evil is attracted to the wounds of our souls. Wounds inflicted from the sins of others or our own personal sins must be dealt with, just as the horse's wound had to be tended to. If that wound had been left untreated, a greater problem would have eventually bothered that horse, and it is no different for us.

I recently purchased a house and began gutting and renovating it along with the help of my family and friends. One day as I was ripping out some boards a nail scraped my arm. It wasn't anything major even though it was bleeding a little, so I ignored it and figured it would go away. I was so busy working I didn't want to bother to clean it or put any ointment on it. I went home that night and took a shower. Because the bleeding had stopped and I was so exhausted, I continued to ignore it. I thought about getting out the ointment and a bandage but opted to just go to bed. As I sit and type this, almost a year has gone by. I can glance down and still see that ugly dark scar on the top of my arm which is a constant reminder that if I had just taken care of it right away, I wouldn't see it or even remember the incident.

I knew that during separation I didn't want my soul wounds to be left alone to heal on their own. I didn't want a scar of ANY kind. Interior scars, left alone, may not be physically seen, but they manifest in unhealthy relationships down the road. Instinctively I knew I needed assistance from a Source greater than myself, just as that horse needed my uncle's tender hand and wise administration. I realized I could allow my own wounds to heal without any treatment, but if I made that choice, the scars would be deep.

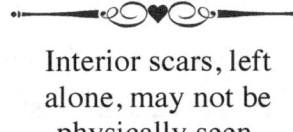

> Interior scars, left alone, may not be physically seen, but they manifest in unhealthy relationships down the road.

As I was processing these thoughts, the African-American spiritual song came to mind, entitled "There is a Balm of Gilead" taken from Jeremiah 8:22 and 46:2, 11:

> *There is a balm in Gilead*
> *To make the wounded whole;*
> *There is a balm in Gilead*
> *To heal the sin-sick soul.*

Soul Wounds: What Are They And How Do We Get Them?

Sometimes I feel discouraged,
And think my work's in vain,
But then the Holy Spirit
Revives my soul again.

I knew I needed to explore that angle further to fully understand exactly how the Holy Spirit heals. How is the Holy Spirit the Balm we need to heal our wounds? How does God heal the soul—my mind, will, and emotions? And if He could heal my soul, would my wounds and scars be minimal? Would my scars go away completely?

I decided to ask God to heal my soul, to be my Balm of Gilead, and I started asking Him to show me how He wanted me to respond to my hurts and negative emotions. I noticed, however, it felt harder to ask God for help than it felt to just respond in my sinful ways. Because we become so accustomed to dealing with wounds in unhealthy ways, we often choose that path, the path that feels easier because it's the path of least resistance. Maybe we try to stuff or ignore our pain, spew anger, eat a bag of chips, or deal with it in some other unhelpful way.

During separation and divorce, many situations can trigger the pain of our soul wounds. Think about how you respond when you are hurt or angry. When someone hurts you, it feels great to spew out the torrent of negative emotions regarding a given situation. You and your friends get your roasting sticks out, pull up a chair at the campfire, and go to town talking smack about your enemy.

Why? Because discussing the entire situation of what someone else has done to you makes you feel better. It releases all your righteous anger. Of course, it feels good to roast someone else when you've been burned. In my sinful way, I envisioned get-even scenarios, fantasizing about God's vengeance being applied. This spew of emotions even felt cathartic in the short term.

Afterward, though, I just felt terrible, angry, and bitter. These outbursts did nothing to ease my pain beyond one brief moment in time. We can pray for God to reveal our unhealthy ways of dealing with our soul wounds. Then we can make a choice to follow Jesus Christ's example in word and in deed. We ask ourselves, "Do I want to lead a peaceful, holy life, or do I want to live life as a bitter, angry, scorned person?"

Can you ask yourself the same question now? What is your answer? Maybe you answered a resounding, "Yes! I want to get better and do things God's way." Or maybe you're not sure yet. That's okay. I know you have this book in your hands for a good reason. As you look for a path of healing, I am confident that as you continue to read and apply these principles, you will begin to heal.

I asked myself those questions, and in the end I decided I really wanted to live a holy life and rise above as a child of the King, a princess! God taught me how to give all my nasty feelings to Him, my Abba Father, to place my pain, heartache, and soul wounds in the Great Physician's hands so that when the healing was finished, there would be no scars of anger, bitterness, hurt, or heartache.

Soul Wounds: What Are They And How Do We Get Them?

In the place of those negative feelings, there would only be deep, abiding peace—possibly an itty-bitty tiny scar—as a gentle reminder of what was and had been. Those scars represent where we've been, so we do not repeat the same mistakes. Those marks are pieces of evidence of sorrows and trials that have turned into character building lessons. In order to get to that place of peace, though, I had to go against the grain, to stop seeking the quick fix to kill my pain. I had to die to my flesh and yield to the Holy Spirit.

The Choice to Yield to the Spirit or to the Flesh

We always have a choice to yield to the Holy Spirit or to yield to the flesh. Yielding to the Holy Spirit means dying to ourselves. It is the act of letting His spirit fill our soul and override the natural tendencies of the flesh. According to Galatians 5:17, *"For the flesh lusteth against the spirit, and the spirit against the flesh: and these are contrary the one to the other: so that ye cannot do the things that ye would."* We see here there is a battle raging between the flesh and the spirit. Where does that leave the soul?

Let's imagine this: our soul (the mind, will, and emotion) is in the middle; it is filled up from either the flesh side or the spirit side of who we are. How our souls are filled is what gives direction to our mind. The choice of where to focus our minds affects our emotions and causes our will to move in one direction or the other. According to the Scriptures, if we allow our minds to be filled with the flesh, we will sin. When we allow our minds (our souls) to be filled with the Spirit, we will respond in godly ways and find healing. A Biblical principle is found in this quote by Dianna Kokoszka which says, "What you focus on expands."

When we don't allow the Spirit of God to fill us, our flesh wins out. In 1 Peter 2:11 we see that sins of our flesh fight against our soul: *"Dearly beloved, I beseech you as strangers and pilgrims, **abstain from fleshly lusts**, which war **against the soul**."* What causes the fighting? In part, the wounds inflicted due to sin. When we are deeply hurt by our spouses, trust me, there are some "fleshly lusts" which come out—and I do not mean the sexual kind! In this verse, lust means a passionate longing.

I am quite certain that when a spouse finds out the other is cheating or looking at pornography, the fleshly response is a longing to retaliate in a very physical way with a good old sucker punch! Or, for some, the retaliation longed for will be in the form of "death by whiplash of words." During separation or divorce, learning how to avoid the pitfalls of retaliation is a daily task, and some days it seems like it will be a lifelong task! Hang in there! God promises great rewards for those who overcome.

Let's think about some examples that might occur during separation or divorce. Maybe you get an unexpected summons to be in court over an increase in child support, or you enter into a heated discussion of who is picking up the children, a fight which turns into World War III. Maybe you are confronted with meeting your ex or your spouse's significant other. What other examples do

Soul Wounds: What Are They And How Do We Get Them?

you think of? As those events unfold causing wounds—and rightfully so—which choice do you want to make? We always have the choice to choose unhealthy coping mechanisms— flesh patterns— or to turn to God.

When the Spirit Fills the Soul

I asked you to imagine your soul in the middle with your flesh on one side and your spirit on the other. Let's go back to that concept and dig in a little deeper.

Envision three pitchers each representing each part of us:

Body   Soul   Spirit

(Fleshly Wants & Desires)   (Mind, Will, Emotions)   (Sinless/Perfect Spirit)

What fills the soul is partially determined by the choices we make with our thoughts and emotions. For example, we can think about getting even, inflicting pain, or lashing out. That is the pitcher labeled "body" dumping toxic thoughts into our souls. On the flip side, we can choose to let the Spirit fill our soul. That is accomplished by reading God's Word, praying, singing praise and worship to God. The Spirit fills our souls each time we choose to obey God. Choosing to let the Spirit fill our souls is what will bring healing.

Obedience, or a Spirit-filled life, brings blessings. God desires good things to fall on His people which is why He gives clear direction in the Word of God. Picture a loving, protective mother holding her child's hand when walking across the street. She does not hold her child's hand to bind the child or prevent him from having fun but for that child's own protection. God wants to protect us too! Our Heavenly Father asks us to hold His hand as we cross the emotional highway of life.

> Our Heavenly Father asks us to hold His hand as we cross the emotional highway of life.

Daily blessings are bestowed on us when we follow in His steps, when we listen and obey Him.

Right now, in this painful time, leaning into God as our Abba Father is very important as He steps in and binds up our wounds. Over 2,000 years ago, He took our punishment, so we could be free and healed.

Amazing, isn't it, what Jesus Christ did for us? If He went to all that trouble to give us a way to be healed, shouldn't we take the time to learn what steps we must follow to benefit from that ultimate healing? The steps listed in this book, when applied, will bring healing and peace. This process takes work and is not the easiest way, but in the long run, the rewards far outweigh any temporary discomfort. If we faithfully take every single soul wound to Jesus Christ and lay it down, we will be healed.

This is a process that may take a while, or it may happen quickly. What's important is that you keep turning to Jesus. Only then will you find healing and peace. The peace that will come is what is spoken of in the book of Isaiah 26:3, *"Thou wilt keep him in perfect peace, whose mind is stayed on thee: because he trusteth in thee."*

Soul Wound Principles in the Old Testament

Before we move on to healthy ways to deal with our soul wounds and how to find healing, let's turn to the Old Testament where we find more key Scriptures to help us understand soul wounds.

We're going to look at the concepts of blessings and curses.

Read what happened to the Israelites when the flesh wins the battle and fills the soul:

"But it shall come to pass, if thou wilt not hearken unto the voice of the Lord thy God, to observe to do all His commandments and His statutes which I command thee this day; that all these curses shall come upon thee, and overtake thee" (Deuteronomy 28:15).

Because we don't use the word "curse" much anymore as it has such a harsh connotation, let me give you another way to understand curses. Curses are the consequences of a negative action (sin). Let me break it down a bit. God says throughout chapter 28 of Deuteronomy to obey His commandments. When we obey, blessings come. On the other hand, when we disobey, curses come. This is clearly stated in the following verses:

> *Moreover all these curses shall come upon thee, and shall pursue thee, and overtake thee, till thou be destroyed; because thou hearkenedst not unto the voice of the Lord thy God, to keep His commandments and His statutes which he commanded thee: And they shall be upon thee for a sign and for a wonder, and upon thy seed forever. Because thou servedst not the Lord thy God with joyfulness, and with gladness of heart, for the abundance of all things (Deuteronomy 28:45-47).*

God told the Israelites to obey Him and keep His commandments, to avoid sin, as well as to serve Him joyfully, something I've messed up many times! When the people sinned—they responded in the flesh rather than the Spirit— God, who is righteous and just, had to allow the natural consequences of disobedience to take place. Deuteronomy Chapters 28 - 30 tells us that the Israelites would see either blessings or cursings. The choice was up to them. In the same way, even during the ups and downs of separation or divorce, we have the choice. I encourage you to take a few minutes to read these very enlightening chapters for yourself.

SOUL WOUNDS: WHAT ARE THEY AND HOW DO WE GET THEM?

Soul Wound Principle in the New Testament

A story in the New Testament that helps us understand soul wounds is found in Mark 5:1-13, the story of the man in the tombs. Every story in the Bible seems to have a natural and a spiritual meaning, which is why Jesus often said, "*'He that hath an ear to hear, let him hear'*" (Luke 5:24, Mark 4:9, Matthew 9:6, Revelation 2:7). We must dig deeply into the Word of God to find the spiritual significance of the stories and parables. Let's see what this story can teach us about the effects of soul wounds.

The story begins with Jesus encountering a demon-possessed man:

> *...out of the **tombs** a man with an unclean spirit, who had his dwelling among the **tombs**; and no man could bind him, no, not with chains: Because that he had been often bound with fetters and chains, and the chains had been plucked asunder by him, and the fetters broken in pieces: neither could any man tame him. And always, night and day, he was in the mountains, and in the **tombs**, crying, and cutting himself with stones (vs. 2-5).*

Because Mark uses the word *tombs* three times in this passage, we can safely assume it's important. The origins of this word tell us that *tomb* means "to remind or to recall to mind" and "a remembrance" (*Strong's*). In this passage the word *tomb* has both a literal and a spiritual meaning.

The literal meaning of *tombs*, the place where this man lives, is a graveyard, a place of death; a place, as its origin tells us, to remember the dead.

Let's apply the spiritual meaning of *tombs* to possible situations during separation or divorce' to see what we can learn.

Spiritually the graveyard can refer to hurts or offenses, soul wounds that we recall to our minds, repeatedly. I think of this as **"The Graveyard of Offenses."** I'm sure you, just like me, can think of a number of hurts you've experienced or caused during separation from your spouse. Although it's so easy to stay in this graveyard, it is such an unhealthy place.

Let's make sure we are aware these hurts we carry around with us, inflicted on us by another person or from a sin we have committed, have the power to affect us and become soul wounds only when we continually recall and bring them into remembrance. Just like the man in the story was tormented by living in the graveyard, we, too, can be tormented when we dwell in "The Graveyard of Offenses" by rehashing offenses in our minds.

Many of us replay scenes over and over again in our heads, conjuring up all sorts of different responses or outcomes, until we feel we've made it right. Those thoughts might make us feel great, because they allow us to say exactly what we wish we had said the first time when we were caught off-guard or just didn't have the guts to say in the moment. The problem is that fantasizing about what you wish you'd said doesn't take away what really happened or allow us to heal from it; only God can do that.

Be Aware of Satan's Attack

Maybe as you're reading this and recalling specific hurts from your estranged spouse or ex, you're thinking to yourself something like, *I have every right to be angry and offended!* Maybe you do. By the world's standards, you might have every right to be upset over the hurt, maybe so much so that it still pops into your mind every day, triggering sadness, anger, bitterness, or some other negative emotion. You might even have friends or family encouraging you to be angry.

But how is it working for you to rehash the injuries? Are you finding peace and healing? Let's talk about another reason we have to be careful about rehashing these soul wounds: They give Satan the right to afflict us.

When we hold onto those memories and do not deal with them properly, we give the enemy a stronghold. The root word, stronghold, comes from the Greek word *ochuroma*. *Strong's Concordance* gives the definition which means "to fortify, through the idea of holding safely; a castle (figuratively)."

Through these strongholds, demonic spirits can cause us to recall and remember painful experiences we've endured, possibly many years ago. Memories can be doors to strongholds.

Avoiding "The Graveyard of Offenses"

We can avoid wandering in the graveyard and avoid strongholds by choosing to take to Jesus all our thoughts and emotions associated with the hurts. This is how we avoid tombstone living.

Let's go back to the story of the man of the tombs in Mark and read verse 6:

"But when he saw Jesus afar off, he ran and worshipped Him."

As we continue to look at this Scripture passage, we see that the man of the tombs ran straight to Jesus. He was in a deranged state, yet the God-sized hole in his heart knew Jesus was the Source of his need.

Jesus then cast out 100 demons. Let's finish looking at Mark: 8-13:

For He said unto him, "Come out of the man, thou unclean spirit." And He asked him, "What is thy name?" And he answered, saying, "My name is Legion: for we are many." And he besought him much that He would not send them away out of the country. Now there was there nigh unto the mountains a great herd of swine feeding. And all the devils besought Him, saying, "Send us into the swine, that we may enter into them." And forthwith Jesus gave them leave. And the unclean spirits went out, and entered into the swine:

Soul Wounds: What Are They And How Do We Get Them?

and the herd ran violently down a steep place into the sea, (they were about 2,000) and were choked in the sea.

We, too, need to run to Jesus with our hurts, our offenses, with everything we need to be healed from. Remembering the offense of others and rehashing these feelings of unforgiveness only create more torment for us. Following this path will never lead to healing. On the other hand, running to Jesus does.

What life changes would occur in your life if you ran to Jesus for help? What do you want to happen?

Strive to Have Nothing in Common with Satan

There is only one person in the Bible who never sinned, never allowed a soul wound to cause Him to sin, and that Man was Jesus Christ, our perfect example. In John 14:40 we read, *"'Hereafter I will not talk much with you: for the prince of this world cometh, and hath nothing in me.'"*

Satan, the prince of this world, has no power over Jesus. The reason we know is found in the last phrase "and hath nothing in me." Jesus Christ had "nothing in him" or nothing in common with Satan. Because there was no common ground between Jesus and Satan, Satan could not and cannot control His mind, manipulate, or destroy Him. That is why God says to follow Jesus' example. God knows that having nothing in common with the enemy is the way to victory. We see this played out in Matthew 4, when Jesus fasted for forty days and Satan tried to tempt Him but was unable to get a stronghold in any way, shape, or form. There was nothing for him to latch onto or legally attack.

Strive to have nothing in common with Satan who is full of pride, resentment, bitterness, and anger. Unlike Jesus, unfortunately, there are times when we fail and do have things in common with the enemy, which can give him a place to attack us. When Satan attacks our minds, we need to resist in faith. We must push back and not let him get a foothold in our minds, will, or emotions. If we allow our wounds to fester and let our hurt turn into bitterness and resentment, we will continue to wave a flag at the enemy, like a red flag before a bull, encouraging him to land his wrath and evil curses upon us.

> Strive to have nothing in common with Satan who is full of pride, resentment, bitterness, and anger.

When we continuously talk about the wrongs our spouses or others have done, rehashing them over and over again, we give place to the devil and create that legal landing strip for our enemy. We make a spot for him and his demonic forces. Holding on to old wounds and refusing to seek healing for them are the same as coming into agreement with the enemy; we agree with him that the other person is terrible, ungodly, unholy, etc. We no longer see that person as flesh and blood, as a creation of God. Even Christian people, our brothers and sisters in the Lord, can hurt us, but God commands that we should leave all vengeance to Him. It is not our job to retaliate.

God is our only answer because He can handle situations properly, no matter what the situation is. Wounds happen but it is best to let God, who has never sinned and will never sin, handle them. God has our best interest at heart and knows what we need every second of the day.

While we should not rehash or hold on to wounds, thereby giving the enemy a stronghold, on the other hand, neither should we stuff our feelings. Let me give you one warning about stuffing emotions and not acknowledging our feelings, even the negative ones: to just "stuff it" thinking we have dealt with it by "forgiving and forgetting" is not healthy. It is not beneficial to stuff our feelings away; we must all go through the grieving process. I found that talking with a trained Christian counselor and also a godly mentor helped me constructively deal with the wounds in a systemized manner, and you may find this helps you as well.

Nevertheless, we must take stock of how we continually respond to our wounds. If the memory comes up and you continually reside within the pain, anguish, and resentment causing you great distress, you should put it on your prayer list and talk to God about it. It is something you need to work through. In a later chapter we will dig more deeply into how to properly deal with those emotional holds. But for now, know that you must take your soul wounds to God, tell Him how you feel, and leave them at the foot of the cross.

The Holy Spirit Is Our Aloe Vera

As we walk on this path to full healing, I like to imagine God alongside of me fulfilling the role of the Trinity. God the Father is acting in the capacity of a Parent, giving us hugs and kisses on a daily basis. Jesus is the Great Physician and only through Him can we obtain the healing power of the Holy Spirit. The Spirit lives in our "Spirit pitcher" and is the one who soothes our wounded mind with the healing ointment of love. They all work together for health and healing for each one of us.

Let's dig a little more deeply into how the Holy Spirit soothes our brokenness. Let's think of the Holy Spirit as our spiritual aloe vera. Of course, He is much more than just a medicinal remedy, but this gives us a picture of one of His attributes. Aloe vera is known for its healing properties and is a remarkable healing evergreen perennial with over 200 active components including vitamins, minerals, enzymes, and other healthy, healing elements. It can be used internally or externally, soothing and restoring our bodies to health. It amazes me that one plant can have so many medicinal properties. I like to think the Holy Spirit is spiritually to our souls what aloe vera is physically to our bodies. The Holy Spirit soothes, cures, restores, and calms the pain and trauma in our souls.

Soul Wounds: What Are They And How Do We Get Them?

The funny thing about both the Holy Spirit and aloe vera is that neither one can do its job if not applied. When we get a burn on our body, we have to get the aloe bottle out and apply the ointment to that spot. When we get hurt by others, we need to ask the Holy Spirit to come in and soothe our souls and heal our hearts. We must get out the Word of God and apply it to our mind. God's Word brings healing, as we learn in the following verse: *"Then they cry unto the LORD in their trouble, and he saveth them out of their distresses.* ***He sent his word, and healed them****, and delivered them from their destructions"* (Psalm 107:19-20).

> *"Then they cry unto the LORD in their trouble, and he saveth them out of their distresses.* ***He sent his word, and healed them****, and delivered them from their destructions"* (Psalm 107:19-20).

As we learn to handle our soul wounds in a new and healthier way, we will begin to immediately recognize a wound for what it is, take it to God, and deal with it right away, versus letting it fester and harden in our heart. As our soul heals, every area of our lives will be transformed. Armed with an understanding of what a soul wound is, now we see why it is crucial we give them to God, allow Him to gently clean us up, apply the spiritual aloe, and bring us to ultimate healing.

Let's end in prayer. You can use my prayer as a guide and customize as you need.

God, help me keep trusting in You, even when I can't see how it is going to end, even when I feel like I am losing my faith. God, I need You to help me. Some moments all I can feel is the pain, confusion, doubt, anger, and unforgiveness. Renew my soul in You every minute, every hour, every day, no matter what my spouse chooses to do. I want that peace that only You can give. Silence my doubts and help me focus on moving forward to bringing honor and glory to You. Heal me! Jesus Christ, You are my Great Physician, my Savior, and my God. I surrender my will totally to You. Amen

Healing Tools

Memorize Scripture: *"Beloved, I wish above all things that thou mayest prosper and be in health, even as thy soul prospereth"* (3 John 1:2).

Meditate on the Journal from Psalms: *"Hear me speedily, O LORD: my spirit faileth: hide not thy face from me, lest I be like unto them that go down into the pit. Cause me to hear thy lovingkindness in the morning; for in thee do I trust: cause me to know the way wherein I should walk; for I lift up my soul unto thee. Deliver me, O LORD, from mine enemies: I flee unto thee to hide me. Teach me to do thy will; for thou art my God: thy spirit is good; lead me into the land of uprightness. Quicken me, O LORD, for* *thy name's sake: for thy righteousness' sake bring my soul out of trouble"* (Psalm 143:7-11).

Praise Daily and Often: Praise God for the victory and healing will come. (See Isaiah 42, 43:1, and 55:2-3, 6-7)

Prayer Decree: God, Your Word says to trust in You so, Lord, please show me how to get through this. I am going to put one step in front of the other as I move towards complete healing. I trust in You and I am confident that You will complete the work You have begun in me. I will leave the "how" up to You (Philippians 1:6).

Focused Thought: I will have nothing in common with Satan. I will not allow sin to get a foothold in my life.

Lesson 2

Our Secret Weapon

"You need to stop worrying about your husband and get healed." Those words reverberated in my ears as I hung up the phone. That was the wise advice given to me by my brother-in-law approximately six weeks after my husband abandoned the children and me.

I had been learning about soul wounds, as we discussed in the first chapter, but this was just the beginning of my learning and healing process. Keep that in mind, as you, too, go through the healing process. Sometimes it will feel like one step forward, two steps back. Don't let discouragement stop you. Just keep going!

After the call with my brother-in-law, I threw my hands in the air and said angrily, to no one in particular, "How in the world am I supposed to do that? What am I supposed to do, just snap my fingers and — voila! — I'm healed? Please tell me, Mr. Smarty Pants, how does a person get healed?"

Of course, I never actually asked him those questions, but once I calmed down, I did take my inquiries to the Lord. As I learned to make this choice over and over again, turning to the Lord with my emotions became more of a healthy pattern for me.

In the early days of our separation, hurt, pain, and despair swirled around in a constant pattern. I hoped tomorrow would be better than today. All I could do was pour out my hurt and wounded heart to God. I hoped God would turn this awful wrong into a right, somehow, someway.

I knew I needed relief, a solution to this constant pain. There was no book, friend, or pastor I knew that could give me the answers, so I urgently sought clarity from God. I wanted to truly understand this healing process, so I asked Him to guide me through this maze of uncertainty.

In answer to my many prayers, God took me through a series of lessons immediately following my husband's sudden withdrawal from the home. As we covered in the first chapter, one of my lessons was to understand that I was wounded and how I had received those wounds. For ease in understanding, for you as the reader, I wanted to explain what a soul wound was, yet the very first lesson I received was on faith. I had to determine if I was going to trust God, no matter what.

The Power of Faith

Faith. What a simple yet complex word! Years ago, I often found myself spouting off the definition of faith, declaring what it is and using the Scriptures to back me up. However, it wasn't until I sank into the depths of despair, into a hopeless pit during my separation that I realized the true meaning of faith. No longer is faith just a word. Rather, it is as much a part of me as breathing.

I had no idea that faith was going to be the one constant, the foundation, to my healing process. I learned that complete healing comes when I choose to entwine my heart, mind, and will—my soul—tightly into the very fiber of my Father, my Abba, my Heavenly Father.

I pray that as you read this chapter, you'll learn how to stand firmly in faith in God. As you burrow deeply into the heart of God, my prayer is that your faith will take hold so as the winds blow, your foundation will stand, forever strong.

Lord, I Need a Sign

One particular lesson regarding faith was one that God had to drill into my head over and over again. I remember one night as I was *trying* to trust God He gave me a deeper understanding of faith so that for the first time in my life I was truly able to grab hold of faith in a real way.

It was a balmy summer night, and I was out on my typical late evening walk, along with my dog named Peanut Butter (blame the kids for the name; I tried to persuade them to no avail).

I was deeply troubled at the time. I had been asking God to restore my marriage, and I firmly believed it would be restored. I believed with all my heart it was His will for my particular situation, yet I was seeing nothing to encourage me that it would happen. As I was prone to do, I began to talk to God in earnest. "Oh God," I prayed, "I know You gave me a promise, and I know You will do what You said You would do. I have faith in You, Lord. I really, really do! But, God, I just need a sign! Please just say something—anything! Or send someone to give me a word of encouragement. I just need a sign that Your promise to me will come to pass."

As I finished my plea, I stopped walking and began to laugh. God had said something all right. God often speaks to us through the thought of a Scripture coming to mind, and this was what happened this time. A Scripture verse I had memorized long ago popped into my mind: "Faith is the substance of things hoped for, the evidence of things not seen" (Hebrews 11:1).

I thought I had already learned and mastered this lesson about faith. You see, many years before I had gone through a first divorce. Although this book is about my second divorce, let me tell you some of that story.

Years before, I found myself as a single mother with five children ranging from the ages of one to ten. I had been a stay-at-home mom, homeschooling my children with help from my mother. It was 2002 when I realized my marriage wasn't going to last without help for my husband's pornography addiction and infidelity; these had been common occurrences throughout the thirteen years of marriage. It seemed likely we were headed toward divorce, so I needed to find work.

I began to search for a job with flexible hours, something I could do at night while the kids' dad could be with them. I felt led to get my real estate license and did so by April 2003. The real estate market was hot, and I was doing great. Within two years of being in the real estate business, I made it to the status of a "Top Producer." What I didn't know was that the hot market was going to turn into a very cold market in mere months. The housing bubble burst in the late 2000s, and I went for eight months with no sales; no sales equaled no commission which equaled no paycheck. This, of course, meant I'd have no money to pay for food, gas, or bills.

By this time my first divorce was final. I was trying to homeschool the children two days a week (my mom handled the other three days), plus work a full-time job, mow the grass, and handle all the many tasks of household needs.

Here I was six months into this eight-month stretch of no commissions, with the child support covering only half of our financial needs. I sat down to analyze my financial situation one weekend when the kids went to their dad's. I reached into the filing cabinet to pick up my credit card statement, and as I slowly lifted the statement to double check my math, my subconscious was wishing the $0 "Available Credit" would miraculously morph into $1000. Unfortunately, it stayed the same. I was in dire straits.

My family was unable to help financially, and I had nowhere else to turn. I was eight weeks away from a paycheck, and I only had $20 left to my name. I went upstairs, lay down on my bed, curled up in a fetal position, frozen in fear. My mind was reprocessing every scenario I could think of to rectify this situation.

I tried to sell some products from my home-based business (I was also trying to build a business through network marketing) but had no luck. Now my list of possibilities dwindled to next to nothing. Trust me, since this incident, I have compassion for women who prostitute their bodies. That thought even went through my mind. I was in a desperate situation.

Fear cascaded over me with the force and velocity of Niagara Falls. And I repeated these fears over and over in my mind. If I had no money, I could not put gas in my car. If I could not put gas in my car, I could not drive my clients around to show them houses, and that meant no commission. If I didn't get a commission check, I could not buy groceries, if I could not buy groceries that meant my children would starve. Niagara Falls…A. Desperate. Situation.

Then, through that fog of fear, God reminded me of the verse in Psalm 37:25 that promises, *"the righteous" will not be "forsaken, nor his seed begging bread."* He reminded me that He *"will supply all my need according to HIS riches"* (Philippians 4:19), and that *"He owns the cattle on a thousand hills"* (Psalm 50:10). I just needed to hope, move—get up out of that bed, and know that God my Father would provide—somehow, someway.

I needed to accept the fact that I wasn't going to know HOW God would provide. I just needed to believe in WHO would provide and keep moving. God did provide, over and over. One specific event involved my internet being cut off. At the time, I was with a startup internet company. I knew it was cut off because I had not paid my bill, so I gave them a call and explained my dire situation. I told them that as a realtor, I must have the internet to do my job. If I didn't have the internet, then my fax machine would not work. If I couldn't operate the fax machine, the offer I had in my hands could not get signed and I would not get a paycheck. The man on the phone was so kind and understanding. He told me he would turn it back on until the next day which gave me the opportunity to get my buyer's offer signed that day.

During those scary months with no income, I saw God's hand in many day-to-day events, such as the internet story. I like to believe He stirred up compassion in that employee, and it was His way of sending me another "hug and a kiss."

At the time when God provided, all those years ago, I thought I would always remember those moments and have a strong faith regarding financial difficulties in the future. But that wasn't the case.

Why do we think if we conquer a mountain where faith is needed that we will never have to use that faith and conquer another one? Wouldn't it be cool if it was like being a Scout or an Awana student—pass one test and voila! Come on down…you've successfully completed the challenge—never to take "any tests" again. As Christians, it's easy to feel like we have earned the "faith badge," so we get to move on. I wholeheartedly wish faith worked like that, but unfortunately, in the Christian life, that's not the case. While we can be encouraged as we remember God's faithfulness in the past, we still have to make a daily choice to have faith in the present moment.

Then once again, I found myself frozen, in my mind, unable to move due to the weight of fear that settled heavily on my chest causing panic to well up and overflow. My mind screamed at me: "Just believe, just believe in God." Simple, but not easy. I was not truly putting all my faith in God, *in this situation*.

Remember the definition of faith from Hebrews 11:1? Faith is belief, without any signs, words, or flashing neon lights. Can and will God give encouragement along the way? Of course, but our faith cannot be contingent upon those things. By its very definition, that would not be faith.

This realization was the turning point for me. Was I moving? Physically—yes. I was physically walking yet mentally frozen in fear and anxiety. I had to make a choice and decide that I was truly going to turn my questions over to God. And then in faith, I had to let go of them. I was going to blindly trust in Him. I did not know what the next day would hold for my children and me, but

I knew the Word of God. When nothing else made sense, I chose to place my faith in His truth—no matter what my circumstances looked like!

The Partnership of Faith and Hope

Another word that conveys faith is the word hope. Often times we will use these two words interchangeably, but recently I learned a difference. I realized the word *faith* is a noun—a person, place, thing, or idea. Faith means belief, trust, and loyalty. On the other hand, *hope* is a verb—an act, occurrence, or mode of being. So let's break it down.

We have this thing called *faith* (our belief) in a God in whom we *hope* (anticipate, wish, yearn, or want) will keep His promises. Hope is the action that goes with faith. That is why Paul says faith without works is dead. When we want or anticipate something, we will usually see some kind of forward movement. For example, I am *hoping* to go on vacation. I anticipate that vacation (that thing) by packing my bags and preparing to move. See? Faith *moves* us through hope.

What are you hoping for? Fill in the blanks as you work out your own personal faith walk:

I have faith, and I am hoping _____. I anticipate that (what will occur) _____ by doing the following _____.

Let faith *MOVE* you as you hope in Jesus Christ.

> Let faith *MOVE* you as you hope in Jesus Christ.

Faith Comes When We Hope

Faith is present when we hope for something; when we want something that doesn't seem to be possible but believe that God can make it possible.

Hope is the action word that brings our faith to life.

During separation or divorce, there are so many things we want—escape from pain; restoration of our marriage; for our children not to suffer; for finances to be provided; removal of bitterness and unforgiveness, and on and on. Ultimately, for whatever we desire, we need to activate our faith in God who is able to move in ways we could never imagine.

We pour out our heart's desire, and then trust God to give us exactly what we need, realizing it may not be what we think we need.

God is a gentleman. He will gently encourage but will never force us to choose Him. Yet we must remember that faith is the cornerstone in the healing process. If we want healing, then it begins with placing our faith in Jesus Christ and the Word of God.

Why We Need Faith

There are five main reasons to hold onto faith. Faith in Jesus Christ has the power to do the following:

- Save us
- Move mountains
- Resist the devil
- Heal us
- Please God

Faith will save us. In Luke 7:48-50 we see a woman was forgiven because she chose to have faith in Jesus Christ. Her faith in Him saved her. *"Jesus said unto her, 'Thy sins are forgiven.' And they that sat at meat with him began to say within themselves, 'Who is this that forgiveth sins also?'* And he said to the woman, *'Thy faith hath saved thee; go in peace.'"*

Faith can move mountains. Matthew 21:21-22, *"Jesus answered and said unto them, 'Verily I say unto you, If ye have faith, and doubt not, ye shall not only do this which is done to the fig tree, but also if ye shall say unto this mountain, Be thou removed, and be thou cast into the sea; it shall be done. And all things, whatsoever ye shall ask in prayer, believing, ye shall receive.'"*

While going through a separation or a divorce, there are MANY mountains that need to be moved. A mountain may represent wanting a judge to rule in favor so the kids are safe, a major financial necessity met in a timely manner, or conflict with one or more family members resolved. Whatever your "mountain" looks like… faith can move it.

Faith gives us the ability when we are attacked to resist the devil. 1 Peter 5:8-9, *"Be sober, be vigilant; because your adversary the devil, as a roaring lion, walketh about, seeking whom he may devour: Whom resist stedfast in the faith, knowing that the same afflictions are accomplished in your brethren that are in the world."*

Faith will heal our bodies. Matthew 9:22, *"But Jesus turned him about, and when he saw her, he said, 'Daughter, be of good comfort; thy faith hath made thee whole.' And the woman was made whole from that hour."*

Do you need healing? God says your faith will heal you. Are you believing as this woman did in Matthew 9:22 so much so that she rudely pushed her way through a throng of people to touch Jesus. Are we pushing through the mountains, the pain, the heartache to get to Jesus?

I heard a statement while watching NCIS, I know, very spiritual, right? Dr. Mallard said, "If you are in hell, keep on walking." How many times are we living in hell and we just sit down? We wallow in our pain and misery and refuse to get up and keep walking. The only way out of hell is to keep walking. That is why we must push through the crowded pain in our mind and reach out to Jesus! He is there and He will heal.

Faith pleases God. Hebrews 11:6, *"But without faith it is impossible to please him: for he that cometh to God must believe that he is, and that he is a rewarder of them that diligently seek him."*

Faith has the power to save us from our sins, move mountains, resist the devil, and heal our bodies. No wonder God says it is impossible to please Him without it. Faith in Jesus Christ is imperative to the Christian. Without faith our circumstances will be like the sand at the seaside—as the tide ebbs and flows, it causes our feet to sink deeper and deeper in unstable surroundings.

At this point in my separation all I had left was the tiniest flickering flame of light inside me called hope, hope in a God who is all-knowing and who promised to guide me. So while I still had questions, I decided to pick up my faith instead of throwing it all away.

Body, Soul, and Spirit

Before I go any further, I need to pause and give the Greek and Hebrew definitions from *Strong's Concordance* for words I will use often throughout the rest of the book. We'll look at the definition of the following words: soul, spirit, and heart. I explained this some in the first chapter, but I want to go into more detail here.

The following definitions come from *Strong's Concordance*, the word *soul*, used 235 times in the New Testament alone, comes from the Greek word *psuche* meaning "**breath**...by implication... abstractly or concretely (the animal sentient principle only: thus distinguished on the one hand from *pnemua* which is the rational and immortal soul.) The Hebrew words that coincide with soul are *nephesh*, *ruach*, and *chay* which gives us the concept that the soul is comprised of the mind, the will, and the emotions of a being."

The word *spirit* comes from the Greek word *pneuma* meaning "a current of air that is breath or a breeze, a spirit that is human, rational, and immortal." The Spirit is either dead or quickened, which means joined together and made alive, forever as an immortal spirit.

You will want to always double check the words *soul* and *spirit* with a concordance to make sure which Greek word is being used.

Psuche refers to the *soul* which is the mind, will, and emotions of a person. *Pneuma* refers to the spirit which at death, for the Christian, ascends to heaven if you have trusted in Jesus Christ as your Savior. The translators didn't always translate these two words the same way, so it can be confusing if you do not understand the difference in the definitions.

To confuse matters even more the word *heart* is used to refer to the mind (intellect), will, and emotions (feelings). Heart comes from the Hebrew word *leb* "the heart; also used (figuratively) very widely for the feelings, the will, and even the intellect; likewise for the centre of anything" (*Strong's*). So we see that the words *heart* and *soul* are interchangeable.

Activating Faith

Now that I have clarified the difference between the soul and the spirit, we can move forward. Once I understood that our soul is made up of the mind, will, and emotions, I then realized our soul is where we choose to activate faith. Over and over again the Bible states we are to "in faith" believe. As I mentioned earlier, hope is the movement, the action, behind our faith.

As you read the many great stories of faith in the Bible, ask God to reveal something new to encourage you. Watch how each person who had faith in God hoped for something and notice how that hope moved him or her.

Reading stories in the Bible can encourage us to walk in faith. When I read certain stories, I can't help but pray, "God, help me to be like those in the Bible who showed great faith." My goal is to have as much faith as the Centurion in Matthew 8. I want to please God, and His Word says it is impossible to please Him without faith. If faith is pleasing to God, I want it, and I want it all, not just a little!

When I started to understand the powerful connection between my faith, the wounds of my soul, my spiritual and physical health, I more readily could adjust my thinking. I began to see that when I allowed my faith to be shaken, the enemy could get in and mess with my mind which affected me spiritually and physically. It also affected my prayers for my children and myself (we will discuss prayer in detail in Lesson 5.)

Let's look a little closer look at the power of faith regarding the physical body. I found three stories from the Bible that show an amplified faith regarding healing. This helped me understand the power of faith, our health, and healing – both physically and mentally.

The first faith story is the story of the **woman with the issue of blood**.

(Note: She believed in faith and asked for *personal* healing)

But as He went, the people thronged him. And a woman having an issue of blood twelve years, which had spent all her living upon physicians, neither could be healed of any, came behind Him, and touched the border of His garment: and immediately her issue of blood stanched. And Jesus said, "Who touched me?" When all denied, Peter and they that were with Him said, "Master, the multitude throng thee and press thee, and sayest thou, 'Who touched me?'" And Jesus said, "Somebody hath touched me: for I perceive that virtue is gone out of me." And when the woman saw that she was not hid, she came trembling, and falling down before Him, she declared unto him before all the people for what cause she had touched Him, and how she was healed immediately. And He said unto her, "Daughter, be of good comfort: thy faith hath made thee whole; go in peace" (Luke 8:42-48).

Her faith made her whole! This was a desperate woman who had basically been suffering through twelve years of constant visits from Aunt Flo, if you know what I mean. I am sure any woman can understand why she was so miserable, and she didn't have Kotex or Carefree or anything else at her disposal. After exhausting all her resources and reaching out to every known medical professional of the day, there was nothing more she could do.

Then one day, she heard of a Great Healer. She heard of all the miraculous events where many people had been healed. Hope began to well up in her soul. She heard of the blind, deaf, and the crippled being completely cured. I am sure she had questions of her own that ran along these lines: "Is it true? Should I get my hopes up? How can I find Him? I wonder how much He charges. I don't have any more money. Can anyone lend me some money? If there is even a tiny hope that He can help me, I must get to Him!"

Her hope moved her. Her hope activated her faith.

In the end, she figured out a way to reach Him through all her doubts and fears. Because she believed in Him, she was healed. She had so much faith that all she had to do was touch the hem of His garments, and her life was changed forever. Jesus fulfilled that twelve-year-long hope for healing.

We have so many questions and are full of fear and doubt during separation or divorce. I have asked many questions just like this lady must have:

"How can I make it financially?"
"How can I be healed from such a deep wound?"
"Will my children be healed, or will this damage them for life?"
"Will I ever be able to trust again?"
"Will this pain ever go away?"

I wonder what would happen in each of our lives if we were willing to push through every obstacle to get to Jesus and ask our very own personal questions.

Separation and divorce cause emotional trauma and wounds that go deep into the soul, as we discussed in the first lesson. They may not be seen or felt physically, like this woman, but just like her, healing needs to take place. Healing from those wounds takes great faith, and it takes a deep desire to push forward to get to Jesus. That "pushing forward" starts in the mind.

The second example of amplified faith is that of **the centurion**. I absolutely love this story. I admire the level of faith he had, and it is my desire to have deep faith such as this.

(Note: He believed and asked for his servant to be healed)

And when Jesus was entered into Capernaum, there came unto Him a centurion, beseeching Him, and saying, "Lord, my servant lieth at home sick of the palsy, grievously tormented." And Jesus saith unto him, "I will come and heal him." The centurion answered and said, "Lord, I am not worthy that thou shouldest come under my roof: but speak the word only, and my servant shall be healed. For I am a man under authority, having soldiers under me: and I say to this man, Go, and he goeth; and to another, Come, and he cometh; and to my servant, Do this, and he doeth it." When Jesus heard it, He marveled, and said to them that followed, "Verily I say unto you, I have not found so great faith, no, not in Israel..." And Jesus said unto the centurion,

"Go thy way; and as thou hast believed, so be it done unto thee." And his servant was healed in the selfsame hour (Matthew 8: 5-10, 13).

This centurion cared enough about his servant to seek help and healing on his behalf. This makes me think about caring for others when our separation causes pain for others. When a breakup occurs in a relationship, others are affected, maybe not as deeply, but there is still damage and hurt, and healing needs to take place for them as well. I found that praying for others, including my estranged husband, facilitated my faith and kept the bitterness at bay.

Another example of amplified faith is the case of **the nobleman**.

(Note: He believed and asked for healing for his son)

The nobleman saith unto him, "Sir, come down, ere my child die." Jesus saith unto him, "Go thy way; thy son liveth." And the man believed the word that Jesus had spoken unto him, and he went his way. And as he was now going down, his servants met him, and told him, saying, "Thy son liveth." Then enquired he of them the hour when he began to amend. And they said unto him, "Yesterday at the seventh hour the fever left him." So the father knew that it was at the same hour, in the which Jesus said unto him, "Thy son liveth" and himself believed, and his whole house (John 4:49-53).

This story makes me think about my children during the hardships and struggles of this time. Our children and family members are affected by the hardship separation and divorce dole out. Children especially will be deeply wounded. The terrible thing about children dealing with this type of trauma is that, depending on their age, they may not be able to articulate their distress. Many times, they will find unhealthy ways to cope. Praying and believing, in faith, for God to heal these wounds is crucial for them.

At the beginning of my separation, I was in such distress that I was unable to help myself, never mind anyone else. In time, I was able to pray for others but that came months later. At some point, I gave myself permission to grieve. The grieving process is very private. I learned it was a time to stop focusing on others and take care of the pain I was enduring. That was super hard for me to do as a mom, business owner, and as a general "fixer" of all problems. I just couldn't do it all anymore and survive.

Friends and family surrounded me as they helped me realize it was okay to take the time I needed to heal. I had to surrender my children, parents, and friends and their hurts to God and let Him heal them. I didn't have one ounce of strength to help or encourage another person.

I guess it is best put like this; have you ever been on an airline and they walk you through the safety instructions? One of the safety instructions is regarding the oxygen mask. Their instructions are to FIRST, put your own mask on, and THEN administer help to those closest to you. If you do not have any oxygen, you will pass out and be ineffective.

In the same way, I needed to deal with my pain first. Then as the healing process evolved, I could reach over and help my children. I needed to take time to throw myself into the arms of my Heavenly Father and grab hold of that tiniest sliver of faith. In doing so, I was activating my faith. Later, when I moved into another less raw emotional state, I was able to focus prayer on others.

There were so many concerns and questions I had regarding my children such as, "Should I take them to a counselor? If so, which one? Should they stay in the same school? Is it better to move out of our current home to start fresh or stay where they are comfortable and familiar?" So many pressing issues all at once.

(Hey, side note; it is okay to take a "mental health day" or two… three… On those days, my friends and I like to joke it is okay to talk to yourself. But you truly cross the line if you answer yourself!)

It is normal to have all of these questions slapping you in the face. It is normal to be overwhelmed. I learned to calm myself, to take deep breaths, and to start a list of all the concerns or questions I had. I would take the list to a friend or counselor who would help me sort through them and find the one that was most time-sensitive or most important, in that moment, on that day. We came up with a plan for that ONE concern— One At A Time. Then I would prioritize the rest of the list.

Deactivating Faith

The three New Testament examples in the previous section show people who received healing because they activated their faith. The activation began first with their thoughts, then their words, and finally with their actions. If we can activate faith with our thoughts, words, and actions, then we can deactivate faith as well. Remember 1 Peter 5:9, which tells us we are to resist "in the faith." This implies we will be attacked by Satan. If we can be attacked, and our only weapon against the enemy is our faith, that is the very thing the enemy will go after.

Think of Superman. In the comic books and movies, Superman was a very powerful superhero. He was extremely strong and virtually unbeatable. Anyone who came up against him was no match for his extraordinary strength and superhuman ability. There was no way to take him down unless he came in contact with kryptonite. Kryptonite was a substance that would make him weak and unable to fight back.

Our faith is Satan's kryptonite.

As Christians, we have a source of kryptonite, too.

Our lack of faith is our kryptonite.

In turn, our faith is Satan's kryptonite.

(**Side note:** This concept came to me in March 2016 which I journaled. I later wrote and shared this chapter with a friend in Jan 2018. A few weeks later she sent me a link to a new book coming out by John Bevere entitled, "**Killing Kryptonite**" I had no knowledge of this book nor have I ever heard this man speak. Apparently, God gave the same thought to both of us. It must be a very valuable concept that God wants us to take to heart. The enemy is out to destroy us! It doesn't matter who says it - as long as we get the concept.)

The way for the enemy to win is to try and take away our faith. He does that by making our faith dissipate or become deactivated through fear or other means.

Let me share examples of dissipating faith.

- Walking away from church or godly friends
- Pushing for answers NOW instead of waiting patiently on the Lord
- Making quick, rash decisions
- Giving into depression

Can you think of other examples of dissipating faith in your own situation? Allowing our mind, will, and emotions to be overtaken by fear will strip us of the power of God. *2 Timothy 1:7* says, "God has not given us a spirit of fear but of power, and of love and of a sound mind." A spirit of fear takes away our power, our love, and our good judgment. When we realize we've given in and our faith is deactivated or flailing, we can't beat ourselves up! We must choose to turn to God, repent, and ask for strength to get back on track. **Our lack of faith is kryptonite to us, so we need to hold on to faith at all costs!**

Filling the Faith Tank

Holding on to faith and not letting go can be very hard at times. Jude 1:3 says we have to "contend for the faith." In the Greek, *contend* means "to struggle, literally (to compete for a prize) or figuratively (to contend with an adversary)" (*Strong's*).

We must stir ourselves up in faith on a daily basis. I like to think of faith like a tank of gas, and that faith tank needs constant refilling. Life wears us down, and I have found it is crucial to constantly fuel my faith. I praise the Lord for His Word and for Christian music I hear at church or through YouTube videos, podcasts, TV sermons, and Christian radio. All of these help to refill my faith tank and keep it from running on fumes.

When we fill up throughout the day, instead of waiting for Sunday to roll around, we will find that it evens out our ups and downs. I can literally feel myself losing my faith; my low-faith warning light is always in the form of depression. A seemingly harmless thought leads to a very long, internal, and even somewhat intelligent, debate in my head. It starts out with the problem I have with myself or someone else. The negative things I have about myself or someone else come rolling in like a freight train, drowning out any reasonable thoughts. I spiral down into the pit of self-pity and despair. Surely you know what I'm talking about. Many of us have claimed a half gallon of ice cream, a spoon, and a couch—and wallowed big time. Some of us may have even turned to much worse, such as doing harm to ourselves.

We need to fill up our faith tank so that it gives us the energy to pull us out of those negative, demoralizing thoughts. How do we do that? God gives us a clue in Romans 10:17, when Paul writes that "faith comes by hearing." Hearing what? He continues, "and hearing by the Word of God!" That is how we fill up our faith tank.

Personally, I would find ways to fill up daily and often. I memorized Scripture. I planned and set aside time to get alone with God. I listened to Christian preachers on the radio in the car, I downloaded audio books, I played uplifting music throughout the day. I did whatever it took to keep my faith tank full!

My struggles regarding faith coincided with a Bible study we did at church written by Angela Thomas called *Stronger, Finding Hope in Fragile Places.* At the end of each chapter, Angela listed Scripture references. Since she did not have the verses written out, I had to look them up. I looked those Scriptures up and amazingly enough, they were just what I needed, at just the right time! I grabbed a notebook and started writing those verses down. Somehow, I knew the only way to deal with this raw, vulnerable, shattered soul of mine was going to be through the words of the

Greatest Counselor of all time—God! By the end of the six-week Bible study, I had my notebook filled up with timely, encouraging verses.

Do you think that Bible study was just a coincidence? I believed it was perfectly timed for what I needed most. God promises in Psalm 37:23, "The steps of a good man are ordered by the LORD: and he delighteth in his way." I realized it was no coincidence but a "kiss" from my Heavenly Father. Whenever something like this happens, I call these "kisses from my Heavenly Daddy." He loves to send His love in ways just like this.

We may not be able to see God physically, but when we learn His character, we see Him show up in so many ways.

When I needed help either emotionally, financially, or physically, He was there, showing Himself to me in big and small ways. I encourage you to look for "kisses" from your heavenly Father. You will be amazed at how many there are.

Holding on to Faith

When we remember our faith is going to lead to a holy, healthy, healed, God- driven life, we can find strength to hang onto our faith in Jesus Christ. Never believe for a moment that it doesn't matter if you give in and let go of your faith; really, that is all we have, and it is the one thing Satan wants to steal.

Our faith is the most important thing we have, the foundation upon which everything else rests. We can choose to take hold of our faith, build up our faith, or strengthen the faith we already have. When we let our faith rest on the Word of God and not our emotions, we will have a true peace as Jesus explains in John chapter 14.

When we were looking at the New Testament examples of people who walked in faith, we saw that each person had to make a personal decision about what to do or not to do – just like you and I must do.

During this hard time of change, we have so many questions. How do we know what is right or wrong? How do we know if we should file for divorce or wait? Do we allow joint custody, or do we fight it? Do we stay put or move? Not one of these answers is specifically spelled out in the Bible. Many times, I urgently wanted a big YES or NO flashing on a neon sign to answer all my questions. Instead, so many times it seemed I was waiting for an answer that seemed cloaked in obscurity, never to be revealed. I bet you can relate to that.

When I made the choice to settle down and focus my mind on Jesus Christ, however, I found my mindset became so different. As I allowed decisions to be funneled through the lens of "What would Jesus do?" or "What does His Word say?" then those answers would come to me. Many times, those answers came through that "still small voice" referenced in I Kings 19:12. I had to remind myself that James 1:5 says if *any* man asks for wisdom, God will give it to him. That is a promise and one I relied on often.

Faith is Like Climbing a Rock Wall

In the business world, we often think of success in terms of a ladder, something we must ascend. We might have to climb over others to get to the top, and only a select few can ascend to the peak. Our faith journey is different from that, however. I like to think the movement of a faith-filled life is a bit like the sport of rock wall climbing, with all those twists, turns, and unexpected cliffs and jagged edges. There is no way to make a straight climb up a rock wall. In the same way, we find unexpected events and struggles blocking our climb.

When climbing a rock wall, you need equipment, an instructor, and someone on the ground belaying. There are different ways to belay, but I am referring to a technique when there is a person on the ground. That person belays by exerting tension on a climbing rope so the one climbing has security to keep from falling. "A climbing partner typically applies tension at the other end of the rope whenever the climber is not moving and removes the tension from the rope whenever the climber needs more rope to continue climbing"(wiki, belaying).

In order to make the climb successful, all these pieces need to be in place with everyone doing their job or a disaster can occur. When you are rock climbing, at times, you will climb an easy section; at other times, you'll find yourself under a cliff, trying to figure out how to climb up backward! Then there are times when you'll be on the ground, belaying for someone else. Each rock-climbing experience will be unique, as you see the situation from a different vantage point.

One of the scariest moments in climbing that jagged wall is when you have to shift all your weight from both feet to just one. As scary as it is, if you are not willing to do that, you will not be able to advance.

In the rock-climbing experience of separation and divorce, we have to find ways to shift our weight while keeping our faith intact. We may find ourselves in situations, such as selling our home, giving notice at our job, filing papers for a restraining order, or just waiting…being still…not moving, not fixing, just being still. Things will be different, and insecurity will rise up, but we'll never be able to shift our weight if we do not have faith.

Faith in this situation means holding on to the equipment, which is the armor of God, through Jesus Christ, our Instructor, who is helping us overcome and push through hard moments. The person belaying is a pastor, friend, or mentor God brings into your life to assist during this hard time. The person belaying is also the one who should be fixed and grounded in the Word of God, helping us overcome.

How do we overcome? We overcome by believing that "Greater is He that is in you, than he that is in the world" (1 John 4:4). We overcome by relying solely on Jesus Christ and the Word of God and accepting assistance from other Christians who have walked the same path before us (Galatians 6:2).

Faith Is Like a Can of Pringles

In order to see our faith come to fruition, we have to "press or push through." We can all remember times of doubt. Maybe right now you can think of times you've doubted God or one of His promises in regard to your particular situation. In Genesis 17:17, we read Abraham doubted—he laughed when God told him that at 100 years old he would have a child.

So he doubted, then held onto his faith, doubted, and held onto his faith again many times, but he pressed through the doubts and insecurities. Don't let discouragement lead to giving up completely. That is what pressing through looks like.

The Bible says Abraham "against hope in hope believed." According to *Strong's Concordance,* this reference to *against* means, "above, among, by..." I can't help but picture a can of Pringles, one chip stacked on top of another, nicely fitting together to fill the can. Our faith is like that; hope stacked together to fill up our souls. Abraham *among* **hope - in hope - believed**. Many times, in my own personal struggles, I've just sat down and said, "I quit." Then God would send a Scripture, song, or a friend along to help me back up. I would get up again, in faith with hope, and continue to press through—like one Pringle stacked on top of another.

Sarah also pressed through. When the Lord, disguised as an angel, came to Sarah and Abraham, the Lord repeated His promise that they would have a child. What did Sarah do? She laughed! Personally, I imagine it was more of a snort, followed by, "Yeah, right! Are you crazy?" But according to Genesis 18:12, she just chuckled. Did that laughter mean she totally lacked and abandoned all her faith? No! If that was the case, she would not be mentioned in the great Hall of Faith in Hebrews 11.

I believe that through Sarah, God shows us that weak faith doesn't mean a total loss of faith. God's Word says our faith will be tried. In James 1:2-4, we are told we will go through tribulation, but this will bring about patience, which is enduring.

And Romans 5:3b-4, "but we glory in tribulations also: knowing that tribulation worketh patience; And patience, experience; and experience, hope."

Faith is getting back up and grabbing hold of that sliver of hope that says, "Even though I can't see, I believe." Getting back up is part of pressing through. It is a willingness to shift and to move into the next position God requires of us, without seeing or knowing how it is all going to work out. We move forward in faith and hope. The alternative is to find ourselves crashing to the ground because we tried to do it on our own.

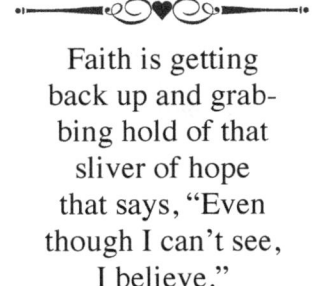

> Faith is getting back up and grabbing hold of that sliver of hope that says, "Even though I can't see, I believe."

As we climb the rock wall of faith, we can't just let go of the rope, stop listening to the instructor, and give up. 1 Timothy 1:19 warns, "Holding faith, and a good conscience; which some having put away concerning faith have made shipwreck," Or else, when we let go of faith, as Timothy admonishes, we could find ourselves shattered against the rocks in the storms of life.

Building Our Faith

Our God is a God of love, and everything we go through is by design. The trials and heartaches we endure are designed to build our faith. Let me share a love story of another woman in another place in time. This is a story of God's design, a tale of Him proving Himself faithful, even when faith was weak. In His great love, God made a way for faith to be nurtured at just the right time:

I'm writing this letter by candlelight. We no longer have electricity on the farm. My husband was killed in the fall, when the tractor overturned. He left eleven young children and me behind. The bank is foreclosing. There's one loaf of bread left. There's snow on the ground, and Christmas is two weeks away. I prayed for forgiveness before I went to drown myself. The river has been frozen over for weeks, so I didn't think it would take long…

As I read that, I can feel the pain that lonely mother of eleven must have felt as she walked down to that icy river, the heavy burden of her loss and sorrow, the unimaginable hopelessness of her situation. I have been there as a single mother of five small children and then again ten years later. I have felt that despair.

OUR SECRET WEAPON

The good news is God had other plans for that mother of eleven, just as He had for me. In His almighty wisdom and guidance, He impressed upon one woman, nine years earlier, to write down the exact Scriptures another would need to hear; the precise words, at that very moment, the perfect time and place, to give hope to one who so desperately needed it. That heartbroken widow and mother needed a kiss from God in her darkest hour, and He made a way for that to occur nine years before that fateful day.

Here is the rest of the story, as told by Dutch Sheets, in *Hope Resurrected*:

In 1965, during a family reunion in Florida, a grandmother by the name of Mrs. Gause, woke everyone at two a.m., issuing orders to get empty Coke bottles, corks, and paper. She believed God had spoken to her in the night and had impressed upon her the importance of people everywhere hearing God's Word. And so she began to write verses of scripture on paper, along with her name and address, while her family, including grandchildren, placed these notes into the bottles and corked the tops. When she felt her assignment was complete, she and her family went to Cocoa Beach and deposited over 200 bottles into the surf.

Over the years, people contacted Mrs. Gause and thanked her for the Scripture verses they found in the bottles. Then, in November of 1974, Mrs. Gause passed away, nine years after the Lord had impressed upon her to send messages of hope in Coke bottles. But that's not the end of the story, for God was still working. One month after her passing, Mrs. Gause received one last letter. This is what it said:

"Dear Mrs. Gause, I'm writing this letter by candlelight. We no longer have electricity on the farm. My husband was killed in the fall when the tractor overturned. He left eleven young children and me behind. The bank is foreclosing. There's one loaf of bread left. There's snow on the ground, and Christmas is two weeks away. I prayed for forgiveness before I went to drown myself. The river has been frozen over for weeks, so I didn't think it would take long. When I broke the ice, a Coke bottle floated up. I opened it, and with tears and trembling hands, I read about hope, Ecclesiastes 9:4, 'but for him who is joined to all the living, there is hope...' I came home, read my Bible, and am thanking God. Please pray for us, but we're going to make it now. Please pray for us, but we're all right. May God bless you and yours, Signed, a Farm in Ohio."

Cocoa Beach, Florida, and Ohio are over 900 miles apart. Not only that, but Ohio is north of Cocoa Beach; things do not typically float *up*stream. Cocoa Beach is attached to the ocean, while Ohio only has rivers. Bearing all these truths of nature and science in mind, think about how that bottle got there, traveling from the ocean to a river, moving upstream some 900 miles! In a word, God! Only through an almighty, all-powerful God could such a miracle have taken place—at the precise moment when it was needed the most.

Forfeited Blessings

One very important point about faith is this: If we choose not to believe in faith, we cannot please God. When we do not please God, we forfeit our blessings. That is a pretty powerful statement and should give us a large amount of motivation. As Hebrews 11:6 warns, *"without faith, it is impossible to please him."* It is by grace **through faith** that God in His mercy gives *"every good and perfect gift,"* to us (James 1:17).

Let me give you an example regarding forfeiting blessings. A forfeited blessing is not saying we did something wrong or sinned in our marriage, so God allowed our marriages to fall apart. What I mean by forfeited blessings is that if God gives you a "Coke bottle" and you choose NOT to open it, or you open it and choose not to accept it, then you lose the comfort or blessing He was offering.

The lady from the farm had a choice after opening the bottle. She could have continued with her intentions of committing suicide, thereby "forfeiting a blessing" of hope and she would not have lived to see faith come to fruition. But instead she did believe, by faith, that God sent that bottle with a message of hope—a message that if she would just hold on, it would all work out. That bottle was God's kiss, a message saying "Hang on honey, I love you. I see you. I will provide for your every need. Just wait. Have faith and it will come to pass."

As the lady on the farm saw the tangible evidence of God's love displayed by a note in a Coke bottle, we also have promises from God's Word we can cling to.

The following are verses I quoted to myself over and over:
 Psalm 37:25," *...yet have I not seen the righteous forsaken, nor his seed begging bread."*
Romans 8:28, *"And we know that all things work together for good to them that love God, to them who are the called according to his purpose."*

We forfeit blessings when we stop believing, when we stop pleasing God with our faith. Wow! That is such simple logic we all need to pay attention to. We do not have to give up our blessings! God has a bagful of gifts waiting to rain down on you and me, if we just believe, as we see promises in James 1:17: *"Every good gift and every perfect gift is from above, and cometh down from the Father of lights, with whom is no variableness, neither shadow of turning."*

Don't give up! Decide to blindly trust in the almighty God. Immerse yourself in His Word. Surround yourself with other rock climbers and hold on to His promises found in the Scriptures. When I found myself slipping into that familiar pit of despair, I would go to the book of Psalms. Part of my healing came through praying the Psalms, the parts that asked for help and the parts that praised God. I would read and pray through particular passages with promises for my situation.

One of my favorite passages of Scripture is Psalm 18:1-6, *"I will love thee, O LORD, my strength. The LORD is my rock, and my fortress, and my deliverer; my God, my strength, in whom I will trust; my buckler, and the horn of my salvation, and my high tower. I will call upon the LORD, who is worthy to be praised: so shall I be saved from mine enemies. The sorrows of death compassed me, and the floods of ungodly men made me afraid. The sorrows of hell compassed me about: the snares of death prevented me. In my distress I called upon the LORD, and cried unto my God: he heard my voice out of his temple, and my cry came before him, even into his ears."*

"Can I blindly trust God?" I pondered. I was in a season where God was trying my faith, and it was the foundation for so many lessons to follow. First, I had to settle this issue of choosing faith in God or not. I searched my heart and knew that no matter what, He is my God, the One I choose to believe in. I hope you will make the same choice.

Healing Tools

Memorize Scripture: Hebrews 11:6, *"But without faith it is impossible to please him: for he that cometh to God must believe that he is, and that he is a rewarder of them that diligently seek him."*

Meditate on the Journal of Psalms: Psalm 6: 6-7a, *"I am weary with my groaning; all the night I make my bed to swim; I water my couch with my tears. Mine eye is consumed because of grief."*

Praise Daily and Often: Praise God that He is your strength and place of safety. God is your "refuge and strength, a very present help in trouble" (Psalm 46:1).

Prayer Decree: Today, in this moment, I believe in the Creator God. I believe He will do what He promised in Philippians 1:6. I am *"confident of this very thing, that He which hath begun a good work in [me] will perform it until the day of Jesus Christ."* I don't know how, and I don't know when it will all work out, but if I have to believe in anything, I believe in God! God, you are my strength, my refuge. I trust in You to get me through the next five minutes.

Focused Thought: Remember what God can and will do, not what man can't or won't do.

Lesson 3

Dealing with a Liar

One of my biggest struggles during separation was trying to figure out the answer to a simple question: *Why, God? Why did my husband decide he "needed a break from the kids and me?"* This was the only explanation he gave me. We enjoyed each other's company, we loved the same things, believed the same things, and communicated well. There was very little arguing or fighting, as we were typically on the same page. The occasional arguments we did have surrounded the discipline of the children—something that is common across the board in most families, blended or otherwise. We were dedicated Christians who knew the Word of God.

From the outside looking in, we had it all together, and from my point of view, life was good. So, what did I miss? Why was he saying he needed this break? I didn't have all the answers, but very early on, God showed me a large part of the why.

A lesson God wanted me to learn was that we all have an enemy, and that enemy's cruel mission is to kill, steal, and destroy (John 10:10) by any and all means necessary. What does he want to kill, steal, and destroy? Our lives—and that typically begins with our families.

Unfortunately, a Christian couple goes straight to the top of the enemy's "most wanted" list the moment we say, "I do." Why? Because the enemy is not a fool; he knows if he can fracture the very nucleus of a family, not only will the couple be harmed, but he will also be able to indirectly dig his claws into the children and extended family. Separation or divorce affect so many people's lives, like a ripple in a pond, if not a tsunami.

Christians do not have just one enemy; we actually face three enemies: the world, our flesh, and the devil. The *world* is a reference to the nonbelievers we come in contact with every day. These people could be our family, neighbors, bosses, or acquaintances. Nonbeliever refers to anyone who does not believe in God and Jesus Christ as his or her Savior.

> Christians do not have just one enemy; we actually face three enemies: the world, our flesh, and the devil.

The enemy in the form of our *flesh* refers to the wants and needs of our physical bodies, such as food, sleep, sex, material possessions, or wealth. It isn't too difficult to see how our entitled, selfish flesh works against us. We see strong evidence of the work of the flesh in all kinds of forms, including unfaithfulness, during separation or divorce.

The enemy who we do not so easily understand is *Satan*. We all have some basic ideas about him, but it's always best to seek the wisdom of the Scriptures to eliminate any mistaken assumptions.

God gives a starting point for understanding the attacks of Satan in Hosea 4:6. God says, *"My people are destroyed for lack of knowledge."* If we can be destroyed due to a lack of knowledge, we can be protected when we seek knowledge. In this day and age, with the Word of God literally at our fingertips, right there in cyberspace on our cell phones, laptops, and numerous other electronic devices, along with the printed Word, this is a pretty easy fix. We are very privileged to live in this time where we can continue to seek knowledge. Let's delve into Scripture to gain knowledge about the enemy, Satan.

Our Greatest Enemy

Biblical knowledge about Satan and the fallen angels we know as demons prepares us to avoid many pitfalls and make life smoother. Bear with me as we go down this road, as I promise to clearly show why this knowledge matters during a separation or divorce. I will explain how the enemy affects us by using our pain and soul wounds caused by broken relationships.

In the beginning, Lucifer was an angel, but when he tried to exalt himself and be like God, he was cast out of Heaven. *"How art thou fallen from heaven, O Lucifer, son of the morning! How art thou cut down to the ground, which didst weaken the nations! For thou hast said in thine heart, I will ascend into heaven, I will exalt my throne above the stars of God: I will sit also upon the mount of the congregation, in the sides of the north: I will ascend above the heights of the clouds; I will be like the most High"* (Isaiah 14:12-14).

We know from Revelation 12:7-9 that when Lucifer was cast out, he took one-third of heaven's angels with him, and we know them as demons: *"And there was war in heaven: Michael and his angels fought against the dragon; and the dragon fought and his angels, and prevailed not; neither was their place found any more in heaven. And the great dragon was cast out, that old serpent, called the Devil, and Satan, which deceiveth the whole world: he was cast out into the earth, and his angels were cast out with him."*

Knowing where Satan went after being cast out of heaven will help us understand the havoc he created in the past and today. The first reference of Satan was in the Garden of Eden, but where did he go after that?

A second reference to Satan is found in Job 1:7, *"And the Lord said unto Satan, 'Whence comest thou?'* Then Satan answered the Lord and said, *'From going to and fro in the Earth, and from walking up and down in it.'"*

A third reference shows up in the Gospels when Jesus was being tempted in the wilderness. Satan was carousing, walking *"to and fro in the earth...up and down in it"* creating destruction and chaos all around. From the book of Genesis and through to the book of Revelation, we see Satan has been bouncing back and forth from heaven to earth since the Garden of Eden and will be here until the end of the earth as we know it.

Dealing with a Liar

Our enemy, Satan, is known by many names. Lucifer was his name when he was created. He once had pleasant sounding names, such as the Angel of Light and Anointed Covering Cherub. Later, he was rightfully dubbed with many other frightening names, such as the Dragon, Serpent, The Evil One, Prince of the Power of the Air, The Devil, Deceiver of the World, The Beast, a Roaring Lion, the Father of Lies, an Adversary, and an Accuser of the Brethren (*Strong's*).

I want to zero in on three specific names for a moment: "The Father of Lies," "adversary," and "the accuser of the brethren."

The first specific name I would like to mention is "The Father of Lies." We get that nickname for Satan from John 8:44 where is says, *"He was a murderer from the beginning, and abode not in the truth, because there is no truth in him. When he speaketh a lie, he speaketh of his own: for he is a liar, and the father of it."*

Understanding that Satan is the father of lies and that anything coming from his side of the aisle will be a lie is a foundational truth we must understand as we seek complete healing. Truthful words heal, false words tear down. In order for healing to take place we have to "put on" the Medicine of Truth. Deciphering between truth and a lie can be hard, at times. As you continue to read this chapter, I want to share the enemy's "playbook" so you can unmistakably distinguish between the two.

The second specific name given to Satan I would like to review is "our adversary," a term that comes from a stern warning in 1 Peter 5:8. *"Be sober, be vigilant; because your adversary the devil, as a roaring lion, walketh about, seeking whom he may devour."* According to *Strong's Concordance*, the Greek word adversary is *antidikos* (an-tid'-ee-kos), and it is defined as "an opponent (in a lawsuit); especially, Satan (as the arch-enemy)." Satan is our legal opponent. Hold onto this information because it is crucial to understanding how Satan can affect us when our souls are wounded, when we are vulnerable, susceptible to attack in our weakened state during separation or divorce.

The third specific name given to Satan I'd like to delve deeply into is "the accuser of the brethren," as we see in Revelation 12:10. *"The accuser of our brethren...accused them before our God day and night."* The Bible says he stands day and night

DEALING WITH A LIAR

accusing. Job 1:6 says Satan presented himself before God, *"Now there was a day when the sons of God came to present themselves before the Lord, and Satan came also among them."* I can't help envisioning the courtroom in heaven much like we see it today on earth.

In Verse 11 of Revelation 12, we read that Satan accused those who *"overcame him [Satan] by the blood of the Lamb, by the word of their testimony; and loved not their lives unto death."* He accused the children of God by bringing legitimate sins, transgressions, and iniquities before God in a courtroom setting. Satan knew God was a just and righteous judge, and as the ultimate authority, He must answer these legal complaints.

Before we can walk in victory, we must understand this role Satan plays. He is our adversary and our accuser. One day he will be cast down from his position as accuser, but for now, he comes into Heaven, serving as the prosecutor against the saints of God. Revelation 12:9 gives a glimpse of Satan's future: *"for the accuser of our brethren is cast down, which accused them before our God day and night."* This is future prophecy; he is not cast down yet, but he will be. At this present moment, even as you are reading this page, Satan is still roaming the earth looking for accusations to bring against Christians. He is in full force in his job of *"seeking whom he may devour,"* and whenever he discovers sin, he gleefully goes back to the courtroom of Heaven to present his case, get a verdict, and apply the punishment.

I always wondered why Satan hated Jesus so much and why he was so bent on destroying what God loved. Lucifer was created to serve Jesus, yet instead of fulfilling his God-given role, he yearned to take Jesus Christ's place and *be* served. He rebelled against the role he was created to fulfill, as found in Jude 1:6a, *"And the angels which kept not their first estate, but left their own habitation...."* He chose instead to leave his created place. He then attempted to get Jesus to sin and take Him down along with anything and anyone He loves—namely, you and me.

Satan had it all, but he rejected it and instead seeks to destroy us because of our relationship with Jesus Christ. Because we are children of God, we are Satan's enemy. He will take every opportunity to drive a wedge between God and us because he is jealous of our relationship with the very God he turned his back on. This may seem childish. However, unlike a child, Satan is crafty and clever. In Ezekiel 28, the entire chapter talks about him. He is referred to as the prince of Tyrus, and in verse 13 we see that he was in the Garden of Eden. That is how we know this Scripture is not just referring to a man. This makes him a powerful enemy. To be found in the crosshairs of an enemy as powerful as Satan is a position we need to avoid.

We learn to avoid the crosshairs by building and maintaining our faith, along with understanding how the enemy targets us and uses our soul wounds against us.

Sporting Sensational "Spiritual" Glasses

Given that we have a very real enemy, one who is sly, we must decipher how to be wise in navigating life while so many darts are thrown our way. Ephesians 6:16b says we are to take *"the shield of faith, wherewith ye shall be able to quench all the fiery darts of the wicked."* Satan is going to throw spiritual darts of fire. However, we can block his attempt to bring us down by holding up the shield of faith.

Demonic forces want us to stay broken, unhealthy, and festering with soul wounds that never heal. If we do not fully heal, our ability to help ourselves and others will be limited and ineffective. If the enemy succeeds at hiding us under his proverbial thumb, we cannot be the light we were intended to be, bringing God the glory, a goal which is our reason for living.

The Old Testament is filled with true stories of both good and evil being knocked down or advanced. Some people we read about in the Old Testament used the shield of faith successfully while others did not. I'd like to share a few stories that may help you gain perspective on how to be spiritually intuitive. Before we can fully heal, we have to understand the roadblocks set up to stop our ultimate recuperation and recovery. These roadblocks are designed by our enemy to cause us to fail.

As you read these stories, imagine you are now wearing sensational spiritual glasses with laser lenses which allow you to glimpse into the parallel spiritual story going on behind the scenes. Put on your top-of-the-line, one-of-a-kind, spiritual glasses and peek into that invisible world. Wearing these "spiritual glasses" will help you become aware of the raging spiritual battles people faced in the past and how you continue to face them now.

Understand that even though we don't see Satan or his demons mentioned in the following stories of the Old Testament, we clearly see their handiwork. Below are great examples of how to live in defeat or victory, in both the natural and the spiritual worlds. When we keep that as our focus while we read, the Bible will come alive like a Steven Spielberg movie. That is precisely why it is called the living, breathing Word of God!

My Story

In February of 2015, my husband and I were at a church service, and we felt prompted by the Lord to go forward during the invitation because we believed God was calling us into ministry to help blended families. We did not know exactly the what, when, or where, but we knew God had placed a calling on our life we needed to fulfill. In March, one month later, my husband's old high school girlfriend reached out to him through Facebook. By November of that same year, my husband had left the children and me. My husband had told me she reached out, and he was curious as to why. He said he was just going to see what she wanted. I didn't hear any more and totally forgot about it since

Dealing With A Liar

I trusted him completely. Unbeknownst to me, the relationship continued from just "catching up" to something more. Can you see evil at work here? Clever, wasn't it? Something seemingly so innocent used as a way to trap a person.

Who benefited the most from our separation: God or Satan? I sensed God showing me right away what was happening, clearly revealing that Satan was on a mission to stop our ministry, a feat he accomplished by causing the breakdown of our marriage. The devil is well aware of a principle we find in Ecclesiastes 4: 9-12, *"Two are better than one; because they have a good reward for their labor. For if they fall, the one will lift up his fellow: but woe to him that is alone when he falleth; for he hath not another to help him up. Again, if two lie together, then they have heat: but how can one be warm alone? And if one prevail against him, two shall withstand him; and a threefold cord is not quickly broken."*

God, husband, and wife are a threefold cord that is not easily broken. Being together in unity is very powerful. That is why the job of the enemy is first to divide and then to conquer. That has been the theme of warfare ever since the serpent approached Eve in the Garden of Eden. It is rather a clever scheme that worked back then and still works today. You see, we could not be in ministry when our own family was crumbling to pieces. In fact, we couldn't do much of anything except just get through the day, one step at a time, trying to make it through the next five minutes, the next hour, the next day.

My Journal Entry:

The following journal entry taken from my actual journal at the time shows the havoc:

---

*"I am coming to grips with the fact that my husband is gone. I was expecting him to come home and when that didn't happen, I began to spiral downward again. Then a friend shared a book with me entitled, **When Godly People Do Ungodly Things**, by Beth Moore. It couldn't have come at a better time, as it was the perfect message for me. Lately, my mind has been a whirlwind of fear, anxiety, confusion, anger, and despair. Every worst-case scenario has been played out in my head over and over again. I know it is spiritual attack, but that doesn't keep me from wanting to run away, from wanting to shove my head under the covers and never come out."*

During a separation or a divorce, our emotions and thoughts will be all over the place, as you can see from my journal entry. Learning about spiritual attack and more importantly, learning how to fight against it, changed me so much and allowed me to move toward healing.

Seeing our circumstances through God's wide-angle lens is imperative if we are going to stand and resist the devil as God commands us to do. We must see things with spiritual eyes and be aware of the "wiles of the devil." I had always heard about those tricks, but now I had a front-row seat to see them played out in my own life.

Once we understand there is an evil force, namely Satan and his fallen demonic angels, we can combat the true enemy. You see, often when we are hurt and betrayed by a spouse, that person seems like our enemy. Recognizing that the true enemy is Satan completely changes the playing field.

Even in the midst of my pain, by using my spiritual glasses I recognized the enemy at work. I believe if my husband had done the same and recognized spiritual attack, he could have guarded his heart. He naïvely thought he could "just catch up" with an old girlfriend, an act which seemed innocent enough at the time, right? If he had been wearing his spiritual glasses, perhaps he would have seen the trick of Satan coming across his computer screen. Perhaps he would have blocked her and told me about it, thereby creating an accountability partner, keeping the three-fold cord nice and tight. If that had been the case, our story could have had a very different ending.

The Story of Abraham and Sarah

Going to the Scriptures for examples of spiritual warfare is helpful because we can see the whole story from start to finish. Think of it like being a "Monday morning quarterback." Just as football coaches and players examine the "plays," we should, too, so the next time we "take the field" of life we have a deeper understanding of common mistakes. Hopefully, by spotting them in others' lives, we can more readily avoid them in ours.

One story where we find evidence of the work of Satan is the story of Abraham and Sarah. They were promised that Abraham would be the father of many nations, a direct promise from God. Then along comes the enemy, trying to compromise God's promise.

Read the accounts in Genesis 12:10-20 and Genesis 20:1-7 on your own, and I will recap them.

First, let's go into a little background on Abraham. He was a very wealthy and influential man who was known throughout the region. The kings of each area were informed whenever he moved to another location. Much like when our president, prime ministers, ambassadors, or heads of state travel to different countries, they are welcomed and taken care of when they arrive. The royal carpet is rolled out and the world is informed.

In these two incidences, Abraham's arrival was noted, and there were preparations for a meeting with the ruling king. In each case, Abraham told his wife, Sarah, to lie and say she was his sister. She was, in fact, his half-sister but she was also his wife. Even though Satan was not specifically mentioned, we see his handiwork present; he is known as the *"father of lies"* (John 8:44).

Apparently, Sarah was a beauty; think of your favorite TV and movie actress—Eva Mendes, Halle Berry, Jennifer Lopez, or Angelina Jolie. All these ladies are knockouts, and many men would no doubt go to great lengths to be with them. Back in Abraham's day, if a king wanted a woman as beautiful as that, and another man was standing in the way, many times the king would just kill that

DEALING WITH A LIAR

man to get her. Abraham did not want to be killed, so he told Sarah to lie. It was a "half-truth" and in Abraham's mind, justifiable. She was his half-sister, but she was very much his wife. (In Abraham's day there was no law against marrying family members, so it was an acceptable practice.)

On two separate occasions (Genesis 12:12-13 and Genesis 20:2) two separate kings took Sarah. Abraham and Sarah knew there was a high chance that each king would sleep with Sarah; after all, few other reasons would convince a man to barter and trade for a beautiful woman. I would like to think Abraham gave Sarah up only as a stall tactic until he could find a way to get her released. In both cases, God intervened and even though the kings took Sarah, God protected her. She was released back to Abraham, untouched, in both cases.

In these two similar scenarios, if Abraham and Sarah had been wearing their spiritual glasses, perhaps they might have seen the situation differently. Maybe they would have realized the lies they told were not of God but of Satan. They knew there was a chance if they were killed by either king, that God's promise that Abraham would be a father of many nations could not have been fulfilled, right? So logically, we see God would protect them so His promise could come to fruition. Trusting and fully relying in faith on God was a choice they chose not to make.

Clearly, the couple was only seeing things in the natural, not through a spiritual lens. As a result, they were driven by fear, and that caused them to lose sight of perspective and their promise from God. That promise said Abraham would be the father of many nations. If we look back now with our spiritual glasses on, we can clearly see Satan's tactics. If Satan could cause Sarah to get pregnant around the time either of the kings had her in their possession, the promise would have been contaminated with doubts. If Sarah slept with the either of the kings, they would be cursed to wonder if Sarah's child was truly Abraham's son. They didn't exactly have access to DNA testing in those days!

Do you see how fear moved instead of the spirit of power, love, and sound mind promised in the Word of God? (2 Timothy 1:7). When our marriages break down, we too start to live in fear. Our perspectives on life will be skewed. That's why asking God to give us spiritual glasses to see clearly is imperative to healing.

Financial difficulties will come up, decisions will need to be made about the children, and living arrangements must be discussed. Anytime we are struggling and we hear ourselves say, "I'm scared" or "I'm afraid if I do this…then that will happen" then we know we are leading with fear. Praying and asking God to give us a spirit of love, power, and sound mind will radically change the way we respond and help our souls mend.

We need to put on our spiritual glasses to "see" what is going on in the invisible world. Satan and his demonic cohorts are clever and crafty and dangerous as they whisper lies that penetrate our minds, just as they did Abraham and Sarah. What makes them

DEALING WITH A LIAR

even more dangerous is that they have only one mission: to destroy entirely what God holds dear. They know they can't beat God, so the next best thing is to destroy what He loves, which is mankind, you and me. Because Abraham and Sarah did not trust in God, their promised child was long delayed. Sarah could not get pregnant for many months of being in the household of the kings. This should serve as a reminder to us that we must be very careful not to trust in our own wisdom and protection or even logic. This could cost us the fulfillment of a promise, or it could delay a blessing God has in store for us.

As time went on, with Abraham and Sarah still trying to do things their own way, they began listening to the lies of the enemy who stirred them up as they saw the hands of time marching aggressively forward. God's promise of a child had still not come to pass, so they decided "to help" God out by allowing Sarah's servant to become the surrogate mother.

How do we know this was driven by the enemy? Isaiah 26:3 says that if we trust in God, He gives us a *"perfect peace."* I do not know about you, but knowing my spouse is planning on having intercourse with another person would not bring me a whole lot of peace! Nevertheless, Hagar was given to Abraham, and she became pregnant with Ishmael, a story you can read in Genesis 16. It is understandable from a human perspective why they went about things this way. God said Abraham would be the father of many nations, but at this point, both he and his wife were over eighty years of age, and Sarah had gone through menopause. There was no earthly, rational, or biological way she could bear the promised child.

If a woman of that age believed such a thing in today's world, she'd be laughed right out of the church. "There, there, dear," most of us would say, patting her on the head. "Surely, God didn't mean it literally." We might even tell her that maybe God's promise wasn't about a physical child, but He gave her all these "spiritual" children from the Sunday school class she taught. That was how He fulfilled His promise to her. We would kindly and patiently explain that women of her age just simply could not get pregnant, let alone give birth. We might pity her, assuming her dream would not come true or that she was delusional.

Like many of us, Abraham and Sarah fell into the traps of doubt and urgency. They listened to those whispers inside their heads telling them they had to fix it, warning them that time was running out, saying, "God must want you to figure out another solution." Abraham and Sarah did exactly what most of us would do. They looked for a way to help God with His promise, the one He gave them, and we all know how that worked out because the results of that ill-conceived decision are still being played out in the Middle East today. Talk about a ripple in the pond! This one was a true tsunami that spanned millennia and oceans!

How many times have we chosen to take things into our own hands? While going through a separation and possibly a divorce, we run on fear and want to "fix" everything. I know that when I have attempted to do so, it goes about as well as trying to put toothpaste back into the tube. Every time we are confronted with a conflict in the natural world, we need to ask ourselves what could possibly be the benefit for God or for the enemy? As we start training ourselves to view life events wearing spiritual lenses, our actions and decisions will become crystal clear.

I once heard a story of a woman whose husband told her he wanted a divorce. She looked at him, calmly took her wedding ring off, and dropped it in the bowl on the entranceway table. She looked at him and said, "Go, that ring will sit right there until you put it back on me." She didn't try to fix him, their marriage, or anything. She let him walk out the door. Five years later he walked back in, retrieved the ring from the bowl, and put it back on her finger.

So many questions ran through my mind when I heard that story. I wanted to know why he was leaving, what caused him to come back, and how did she manage to deal with everything for the next five years. What she did took courage, boldness, and faith. She put on her spiritual glasses and realized there was a bigger picture. Her husband was struggling with his own issues that had nothing to do with her. God said He hates divorce, but human nature often takes over making it impossible to avoid. This lady allowed her husband to choose the path of divorce but also left a door open if he wanted to do it God's way.

Not all stories have a happy ending like this. I am not sure where you are in your marriage. The door may be slammed shut, or there may be an option to keep the door open. I encourage you to put on your spiritual glasses. See what the enemy has to gain by this separation or divorce. Consider what other options may be present.

The Story of Joseph

The second story we'll look at to see the workings of spiritual warfare is the story of Joseph found in Genesis chapters 37 and 29-46. I encourage you to read the Bible story'.

Joseph was approximately sixteen-years-old when he was sold into slavery into Potiphar's house in Egypt. This situation was an about-face from where he had been at fifteen-years-old. Joseph was the eleventh son of a very wealthy and well-known man in the country. His father had married two women plus two concubines, and Joseph was the first-born son of his father's favorite wife. Because of the favoritism shown to him, his half-brothers hated him, but they tried to rein in their disgust and irritation out of respect for their father.

One day Joseph's father sent him on an errand to deliver food and supplies to his brothers in the field taking care of their livestock. As they saw Joseph approach the camp, with no father hovering over them, they concocted a terrible idea to get rid of Joseph. After years of living with stored up bitterness, their thoughts and words of hatred spilled over into actions. When Joseph got to their camp, they roughly grabbed him and ripped off the coat his father had especially made for him. It was a coat uncommonly made with multiple colors. It symbolized royalty, and to the brothers, it reeked of the favoritism their father showed him. They despised that coat, and they despised Joseph. These actions were a demonstration of wounds in the soul. Unchecked and unforgiven, those deep wounds turned into feelings of bitterness and hatred. Those emotions made for a volatile situation, one the enemy clearly enjoyed and used to his benefit.

At first, the brothers planned to kill Joseph and throw him in a pit where he was sure to never be found. However, Reuben, the oldest brother, overheard their plan and refused to let the other brothers kill him. He somehow talked them into just throwing Joseph into a nearby dried up old well, thinking he would come back later, once all the hot-blooded tempers had calmed down, and rescue him. Thinking the crisis was over, Reuben left the camp. While he was gone, Judah, another brother, saw Midianite merchants coming down the road. He had a brilliant idea and shared it with the others.

We do not know exactly how that day went down, so I am going to take a bit of liberty and write out what I think we might have heard if we were mosquitoes buzzing around the campsite listening to Judah that fateful day. The conversation might have sounded something like this: "Hey guys, it won't profit us if we just kill him. Let's make some money off him and sell him. Look, here comes a caravan of store owners and they are heading right towards us. Let's sell him! If we sell him, it will at least make up for some of the misery we've had to endure while dealing with this little brat for the past fifteen years! How will his dreams of being our lord and master come true if he becomes a slave?"

The brothers thought that was a fantastic idea. They threw down a rope and hoisted Joseph up out of that dark, dank, stinky, bug-filled hole. Can you imagine the feelings that came over Joseph when he heard them coming to his rescue? Feelings of relief, hope, joy, mingled with sorrow and pain at having been treated so cruelly, must have flitted through his mind. Then the short-lived elation of joy screeched to a halt. Emotions of despair and horror must have slammed into him when he realized his release from the pit was not returning him to life as he knew it. His life was not going back to normal but taking a hard-left turn into the great unknown.

Can you put yourself into his shoes for just a moment and get a sense of what that betrayal felt like? The depth of emotions he must have dealt with in those first few days? What a reality shift! In the blink of an eye, he went from being the favored child to being a slave. Joseph had previously dreamed twice that his whole family would bow down to him. Now, not only were his dreams fading like the road in the rearview mirror, but his reality of being "the Boss Man" was even further away than he ever thought possible. His life had just taken a hard detour down the dirtiest, rut-filled, back road you ever saw, and there was nothing he could do about it!

Dealing With A Liar

I can relate as my story had a similar element of surprise. I had no idea what was coming. One day I was a happily married woman; the next day I was separated – with no warning. Nothing! I was determined to live my life as Joseph did and searched the Scriptures to show me how.

He could have been bitter and resentful and rightfully so; rather, he took the situation in stride and did his very best at everything with a positive outlook. I believe Joseph cried out to God for help much in the same way King David did or we do today. I believe he asked for wisdom because as we read his story, we see continual evidence of wise, godly decisions and actions. Joseph apparently used the spiritual glasses I've been referring to.

Joseph was wise and discerning which led to him being in many leadership positions, even while still a slave. We estimate Joseph was a slave in Potiphar's house about seven years before he was sent to prison for another seven years. He spent approximately fourteen years as a slave before Pharaoh promoted him to second-in-command. During that time, he had to wonder what was going on. When would he see the fruition of the dream he had been given? We realize now that he was in training to be the best servant he could be, so he could transform into being the finest leader he could be. His training as a manager over a whole plantation and then over a whole federal prison gave him the needed experience to run an entire country. He was prepared by God for an exact time, in a specific place, and for a particular people.

For what purpose might God be training you? We all have a calling and a purpose, and to move into our calling and purpose takes training. During separation or divorce, it might seem incredibly difficult to see God's purpose for our lives. This confusion is part of the attack of the enemy.

Take hope in the story of Joseph. God loved Joseph just like He loves you. He will use this situation to bring about good. Your training may not be finished, but one day it will be perfected. Again, only when wearing spiritual glasses can you see this.

Back to Joseph.

During that time of enslavement, Joseph had to make a decision. When his life was not going the way he thought it should and when his dream did not come to fruition, he had to choose to hold on to God's promise or to let go of his faith and his God. He had to decide whether or not to place his faith in God, no matter what the circumstances looked like. He saw no way for his dream to be fulfilled, nor did he know the end of the story. He had to choose between trusting God or trusting his own human instincts. The spiritual warfare in Joseph's life was extreme; nevertheless, he kept turning to God.

God's promises to Joseph came in the form of two dreams. While Satan and his demonic forces are not all knowing, as God is, one of them heard Joseph speak to his father and brother. The enemy knew Joseph was handpicked by God, and for that reason,

Dealing With A Liar

he wanted to do everything in his power to get Joseph out of the picture, even using his own family and their evil jealousy to try to silence and hinder him. His own brothers, his own flesh and blood, were angry and bitter and found a way to rid him from their daily lives. Satan worked in their hearts, and that evil festered until they were ready to kill him. However, his brothers, Reuben and then later Judah, intervened, sending him into a life of slavery. It wasn't much of a silver lining, I suppose, but it was better than death.

We know the ending of the story. Joseph was instrumental in saving an entire nation of people. God revealed to Joseph the meaning behind Pharaoh's dream which foretold seven years of plenty followed by seven years of famine. Joseph used his skill set acquired through years as a manager to coordinate the influx of food when the harvest was coming in by the truckloads! When the famine hit, the stored-up food was appropriately given to those as they had need. Joseph was instrumental in saving the people. God did, in fact, *"work all things together for good"* for Joseph and his family, but Joseph also went through a lot of pain to get there, including being exiled from his home. For over a decade, he didn't get to see his entire family. He endured all kinds of physical hardships, and, later, sexual temptation that came at him in full force.

As we continue examining Joseph's story, let's see how the enemy worked, how Joseph reacted, and how to apply these lessons to our own lives. If we take a quick peek at the sexual temptation Joseph had to endure, we can learn much. It seems to be Satan's ace in the hole, a card he plays over and over again, even in modern times. He does this because he knows it works; our flesh is weak and wants to be pleased and is in constant war with our spirit, as the apostle Paul realized in Romans 7:15. When Potiphar's wife came on to Joseph and tried to entice him, Joseph was most likely in his early to mid-twenties, a full-grown man, and a virgin. It is not surprising that he was tempted, and we can probably safely assume his natural desires for sexual relations caused his body to react against his will. Like anyone else, he craved a sexual relationship, and it would have been so easy to give in, which was precisely why he ran to seek escape from his own desires.

The demonic influences knew they merely had to place a normal, typical temptation in front of Joseph to derail him from God's mission. So many times Satan does not have to do much more than use our natural, selfish tendencies to get us or our spouses to fall. We all have desires and thoughts that are simply natural, and our enemy loves to exploit these weaknesses. It was no different in Joseph's day, but if he had given in for just one minute, his whole life would have changed irrevocably, throwing a wrench into God's plan and timing to use him. It would have adversely affected not only Joseph but also his family and an entire race of people. Joseph could have justified it, rationalized it, and reasoned with himself, thinking, *It's normal, it's just my body's natural drive. I mean, look at her! Besides, everybody does it, right? She wants me to sleep with her, and I'm really just a servant who's supposed to do what I'm told.*

Ol' Potiphar is never around anyway. Poor thing's been abandoned. She's lonely, and she deserves to be taken care of. I know God's got plans for me, but... Hey, my happiness is important, too, isn't it?

It sounds reasonable enough, but it certainly wouldn't have been holy. That is the danger of reasoning in our own hearts. God's Word says we must stay pure and only have sex within marriage. Regardless of the reasons or excuses, sex outside of marriage is wrong, a sin, spoken of in the Ten Commandments and many other passages of Scripture such as 1 Thessalonians 4:3-5, 1 Corinthians 6:18, 1 Corinthians 10:8. We must hold every action, every decision against the Word of God to see what aligns with His requirements, not our emotions. His Word is not there to beat us up, guilt us, or steal all the fun from life; it is for our good, the same way a good mother would keep her children from too many sweets.

I used to tell my children, "It may be tasty for the tongue but not great for the body." Just as cookies and candy are yummy yet not healthy, sexual pleasure is good but not best outside of marriage. God's Word says there is always pleasure in sin for a season (Hebrews 11:25). It may feel right at the time because it consoles and fulfills our fleshly desires, but giving in to those can do great damage to us spiritually, as stated in 1 Corinthians 6:18, *"Flee fornication. Every sin that a man doeth is without the body; but he that committeth fornication sinneth against his own body."*

God commands us to die to self for this very reason because it is for our own good. Many of us have felt the pain that came from sexual sins and can see the damage it has caused. We need to lean on His Word, wisdom, and guidance and follow Him even though we may not fully understand. When we do not heed God's warnings, it causes wounds in our souls.

After examining my story, the story of Abraham and Sarah, and the story of Joseph, we can distinctly see how Satan tries to use our flesh to stir up spiritual havoc in our lives. That havoc can be created from our own issues or the issues of our spouses. Either way, if we don't apply spiritual glasses to each situation we can get pulled into doing or saying things that will lead us away from God and toward sin. Sometimes it is the hardest to see when we are not the one sinning, but when we are sinned against. It is unfair and this creates soul wounds if we allow it. Satan is firing well-aimed darts at each one of us, trying to strike us down. Periodically he is successful, especially when we are not holding up that shield of faith.

Satan used a seemingly innocent relationship to destroy my marriage and consequently ended up wounding me, my husband, our children, and extended family.

Abraham and Sarah allowed the wound of disappointment and desperation to motivate them to do things their own way, instead of waiting on God and placing their faith in Him. They made choices that wounded them, Hagar, Ishmael, and an entire nation of people.

In Joseph's situation favoritism caused deep soul wounds the brothers carried for most of their lives, bringing hatred and resentment to the family, Joseph, and his brothers.

We all receive a variety of wounds, sometimes daily. The enemy will try to use these to his advantage to kill, steal, and destroy each one of us along with our destiny.

If we allow the wounds to stay and fester, the enemy can get a foothold and steer us off course and away from the plan God has for each of us. This is why we need to recognize we have an enemy and understand his plan to kill, steal, and destroy. God knows we are going to be hurt. He knows that our flesh, the world, and Satan are forces against us. God, however, did not leave us out here on earth alone. God gave us protection, called the armor of God. It is up to us to learn all about that armor and how to apply it.

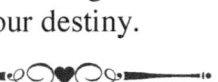

> We all receive a variety of wounds, sometimes daily. The enemy will try to use these to his advantage to kill, steal, and destroy each one of us along with our destiny.

Protection through the Armor of God

As we understand who our enemy is, we see the need for protection. God gives us very clear instructions on how to put on His armor. As we apply His protection, we learn to heal (to stand) and protect ourselves (be shielded) from further wounds. The Bible lists out the armor and the function of each piece in Ephesians 6:11-18:

"Finally, my brethren, be strong in the Lord, and in the power of his might. Put on the whole armor of God, that

ye may be able to stand against the wiles of the devil. For we wrestle not against flesh and blood, but against principalities, against powers, against the rulers of the darkness of this world, against spiritual wickedness in high places. Wherefore take unto you the whole armor of God, that ye may be able to withstand in the evil day, and having done all, to stand. Stand therefore,

having your loins girt about with truth,

and having on the breastplate of righteousness;

And your feet shod with the preparation of the gospel of peace;

Above all, taking the shield of faith, wherewith ye shall be able to quench all the fiery darts of the wicked.

And take the helmet of salvation, and the sword of the Spirit, which is the word of God:

Praying always with all prayer and supplication in the Spirit, and watching thereunto with all perseverance and supplication for all saints."

Once we put on the armor, our only job is just to stand. "... *having done all, to stand. Stand therefore."*

Just stand. Feel the weight of your armor. **Imagine the power of God in your stance.**

Dealing With A Liar

Even though you may feel like you are at war with your spouse or ex-spouse who is poking and aggravating you until you feel the need to pull out every single piece of hair you have left, spiritually speaking, that is not the case. We are not at war with a person or other people but with principalities, powers, the rulers of the darkness of this world, and spiritual wickedness in high places.

Our fight is against Satan and his crew of fallen angels—plain and simple! The true enemy is Satan, even when it feels like the enemy is a spouse who has hurt us. Now that we know who our enemy really is, we just need to get the proper protection.

Each piece of the protective armor has special importance. We have been given full body armor, first made of truth. I always thought the first piece of armor was the helmet of salvation. As I read Ephesians 6:11-18 I slowed down and processed the armor in order. Truth is listed first. Why? Because without truth we have no anchor. Truth is what sets us free (John 8:32). Free to see right from wrong, free to choose salvation through Jesus Christ, free to pick up the rest of the armor and change our lives. It gives us the freedom to be completely healed!

Next, we have righteousness, peace, and the sword of the Holy Spirit to direct and guide us. Then we have our salvation and a shield of faith, which gives us the power to resist and see victory made manifest. Finally, we are armed with the power that comes from the blood of Jesus Christ and His resurrection.

Until separation, I did not grasp the significance of applying these Scriptures and donning the full armor of God. I did not really understand or even believe in the full impact of the raging battle that is daily being performed on our behalf in the spiritual world.

Think about what it means to become a child of God. When we become a child of God, we then become joint heirs with the Son, Jesus Christ. Galatians 4:7 reads, *"Wherefore thou art no more a servant, but a son; and if a son, then an heir of God through Christ."* God is the King of Kings and Lord of Lords, and this verse promises we become royalty—princes and princesses.

In our natural world, the children of presidents, queens, and kings receive protection. As soon as the President is sworn in, a team of highly trained professional soldiers is put in place to protect him and his family at all times. Why? Because evil people out there want to manipulate, kidnap, or even kill our leaders for their own agenda. Evil wants to use them for their own purposes, and those purposes are never for good intentions.

In America, if you became part of the First Family, many changes would take place. You might experience some real Cinderella moments. You would be carted around in a limo by a chauffeur, maybe with your own personal shopper. Staff would be hired to cook and clean for you, so you would never have to lift a finger. Can I hear an "Amen," ladies? There would be other changes as well, such as strict rules about what you can say, what you can

DEALING WITH A LIAR

wear, where you can go, and proper protocol to be observed. Such scrutiny would not be fun, but it would be necessary.

You would also have to come to terms with constant threat on your life. At all times, you would have to live under a heightened awareness of very real dangers facing you and your loved ones. You could go into that situation with fear or with the courage of knowing you are fully protected, surrounded by dedicated, fully trained, well-equipped personnel who would take a bullet for you if need be. At just the teeniest squeak from your mouth, they would come to the rescue. Only if you choose to disregard the Secret Service's instruction or if you step away from their protection would your life be in danger.

As children of God, we can rest with security in the knowledge that although danger is ever-present, we are fully protected if we choose to follow all of God's instructions. Even though the devil, our vicious adversary, seeks to steal, kill, and destroy (2 Timothy 1: 7), God has assigned us a "Secret Service Agency" with Jesus Christ in charge and His army of ministering angels at His beck and call ready to protect us.

As children of God, we have been given power.

> Just as we have a legal system to protect us, as a child of God we have been given spiritual power to protect us.

Just as we have a legal system to protect us, as a child of God we have been given spiritual power to protect us.

We simply have to utilize those legalities we have been given. We need to pick up our rights (our inheritance) given to us as stated in Luke 10:19, *"Behold, I give unto you power to tread on serpents and scorpions, and over all the power of the enemy: and nothing shall by any means hurt you."* The power referred to in Luke 10:19 is such a remarkable Greek word, *dunamis* (doo'-nam-is). This word means "force (literally or figuratively); miraculous power (usually by implication, a miracle itself): ability, abundance, might (-y deed), (worker of) miracle (-s), power, strength, (wonderful) work" (*Strong's*).

I get so excited when I think about what this verse means to us as God's children. Once Jesus Christ rose from the grave, on the third day, that *dunamis*, that power was given to the disciples. The best part is that we have that power in us as well! God granted it to us, and it is how we overcome, because God's Word promises us that *"greater is He that is in you, than he that is in the world"* (1 John 4:4).

There is a force inside of us called the Holy Spirit who lives in us and empowers us with strength, abundance, and the ability to do mighty works and be workers of miracles. Amazing! We just have to believe and have faith. Our faith pleases God because He knows good things come through that faith. Faith and power go hand in hand; you can't have one without the other, and you can't defeat the enemy without both of them.

DEALING WITH A LIAR

You just can't get better protection than the power that comes from Jesus Christ our Savior. Hallelujah! Spiritual warfare is ever-present. But holding onto our faith, applying biblical principles, and saying *no* to festering soul wounds that are trying to consume us will contribute to a holy, healthy life. We can stand strong with the whole armor of God in place for ultimate protection.

It is Satan's job to get us to put down our shield of faith and forget about our armor. It is our job to put on the WHOLE armor of God, wave the Word of God, thereby "resisting the devil" and not giving "place to the devil." Jesus Christ is the "secret service director" assigned to protect me and you. All we have to do is accept that protection.

Let me share with you a great example of a little boy who chose to accept the protection offered by Jesus Christ and the positive outcome that occurred.

The Story of the Little Boy: Jesus Is the Glass

The following is a story taken from Jim Logan's, *Reclaiming Surrendered Ground*. Jim was speaking at a conference on spiritual warfare, talking about the influence Satan and his fallen angels have over human beings. A young boy, Joseph, was in the audience, the child of a missionary in Alaska, who dealt primarily with a people group whose culture was greatly influenced by witchcraft and the occult. As such, the family understood demonic forces. So when Joseph told his father he heard voices in his head the father reached out to Jim and asked him to speak to his son. Below is the recounting of this remarkable story:

Jim was walking with Joseph to speak privately to him when Joseph turned to him and said, "You know, Mr. Logan, I have big problems. Are you good at this?"

Jim replied, "I'm learning."

They sat down, and little Joseph at only seven and a half years old, was ready for answers, with pen, paper, and Bible in hand.

Jim started with a scripture, "You know Joseph, 1 John 5:18b says that when we're in Christ, the wicked one cannot touch us."

"That's a good one," Joseph said.

"Yes, it really is. You ought to write it down."

The boy wrote the verse down.

Jim continued, "Joseph, have you ever been to the snake house at the zoo?

"Yes."

"You mean you went into a snake house?" Jim asked, shocked.

"Sure."

"Really?" Jim asked, giving the child time to really think about it.

"Yes. Why?"

"But, Joseph, there are poisonous snakes in there!"

"Yeah, Mr. Logan, but there's also glass." He pondered that for a moment, and then said, as a smile crossed his face, "Jesus is the glass, isn't He?"

"Yes, Joseph. Jesus is the glass, between you and the snakes."

The best part of the story continued:

"Joseph, what if we stayed at the zoo till dark, and we heard the lion roar as we walked out. Would you be afraid?"

"Yeah, I think I would," he answered.

"What if I reminded you that the lion was behind bars?"

"Then I wouldn't be afraid," Joseph said Then he went on to tell Jim how the enemy had been harassing him with those voices he heard in his head. "

"What did you do when these temptation and thoughts came?" Jim asked.

"I did what my dad said to do. I said, 'In the name and authority of the Lord Jesus Christ, get out of here."

"And what happened then?"

"The spirit left."

Jim explained that he knows about a thousand adult Christians whom he wished could understand spiritual warfare as clearly as Joseph did. The boy wasn't afraid, even when the enemy tried to scare and intimidate him. He said to the child, "Joseph, God must have something wonderful for you to do."

"Why?"

"Because Satan is attacking you."

"What do you suppose God has for me, Mr. Logan?"

"Well, I'm not sure, but He'll show you. Why don't you dedicate your life to the Lord and His will for you right now?"

In a simple prayer, Joseph did just that, dedicating himself to God's will for his life. Later, the little guy ran up to his father, surrounded by missionaries, and said, "Dad, guess what! God has something wonderful for me to do."

About three years later, Joseph revisited Jim and said, "Mr. Logan, I think I know what

God wants me to do. I have a pretty good voice. I think He wants me to be a singer."

Nowadays, Joseph is one of Jim's best pray partners; he has been praying for Jim for at more than nine years!

When we are surrounded by the harsh demands of life and relationships, we can become overwhelmed and scared. Satan is living up to his name as the Father of Lies, attempting to confuse us in a haunted house with glass mirrors, keeping us confused and broken. At times, we will have multiple distorted thoughts that come from the enemy, just like little Joseph. Those thoughts can stay with us and continue to trap us with our soul wounds, or we can give them to Jesus, who takes all warped images away.

The story of little Joseph allows me to comprehend why Jesus says we should come to Him as little children. Young ones have such an innocent, trusting way about them. If we could only remember that when it's dark outside and the "lions" are roaring, or when we are surrounded by "snakes," Jesus is the glass!

As we end this chapter, I'll share one of my actual journal entries with you. I wrote this during a time of feeling weak and attacked by Satan, but I held up my shield of faith to fend off the attacks of Satan. I allowed Jesus to be the glass.

My Journal:

"Everyone says to me, 'You're a strong woman, Valerie. You will be fine. You did it before, and you can do it again.' The thing is…I'm tired of being the strong woman. Why can't the man in my life be strong for once? I know that is not right or fair to think that way, but I do. I know I have to put my faith in God and not in man, but it is so hard to walk that faith out. Those lies the enemy wants me to believe almost overtook me today, but God prevailed! Through God and God alone, and by applying the armor of God, I will stand up and remember Ephesians 6:12 that 'we wrestle not against flesh and blood but against principalities, against powers, against the rulers of the darkness of this world, against spiritual wickedness in high places.' Right now, I feel strong again, but in thirty minutes, I may crumble into the bowels of despair again. Regardless, 'I **know whom I have believed, and am persuaded that He is able to keep that which I have committed unto Him against that day'"** *(2 Timothy 1:12).*

Healing Tools

Memorize Scripture: *"Be strong in the Lord, and in the power of His might. Put on the whole armor of God, that ye may be able to stand against the wiles of the devil… Take unto you the whole* *armor of God, that ye may be able to withstand in the evil day, and having done all, to stand"* (Ephesians 6:10-11, 13).

Meditate on the Journal of Psalms: *"I will love thee, O Lord, my strength. The Lord is my rock, and my fortress, and my deliverer; my God, my strength, in whom I will trust; my buckler, and the horn of my salvation, and my high tower"* (Psalm 18:1-3).

"I will call upon the Lord, who is worthy to be praised: so shall I be saved from mine enemies. In my distress I called upon the LORD, and cried unto my God: He heard my voice out of his temple, and my cry came before Him, even into His ears" (Psalm 18:6).

"Let them [my enemy] be ashamed and brought to confusion together that rejoice at mine hurt: let them be clothed with shame and dishonor that magnify themselves against me" (Psalm 35:26).

Praise Daily and Often: Thank You, Jesus Christ for being my example! You are a wise, all-knowing God who will never forsake Your people or Your promises. You are worthy of all praise, honor, and glory. I praise God for taking care of my enemy. Vengeance is Yours!

Prayer Decree: God, put a hedge of protection around my family. We know evil forces are out to get us because we love You. Please keep me, Lord. When I don't even know how to pray, keep me. Protect my husband, my children, and me. Draw us to You every time Satan and his demons attack. Remind me to hold up my shield of faith to ward off those fiery darts. Help me to keep my thoughts pure and on You (Philippians 4:8). My flesh is so weak. I want to run, hide, and give up, but by Your almighty hand, we will prevail. I don't know the whole picture, the how or why, but I know You will help me, Lord, just as You helped Joseph. Give me supernatural strength to carry on. Show my kids the faith I have always talked about and lived out in this hard time. Amen.

Focused Thought: Focus on putting all the armor of God on, as your defense, yielding the only offensive weapon, the sword of the Spirit.

Lesson 4

Putting it All Together

My Journal:

---※---

"March...My birthday. Wow, what a birthday present – infidelity! I've experienced the ultimate betrayal, and the pain is so great! It's been four months since my husband left and still my mind continues to whirl, wondering what happened. Now I know and with that knowledge comes some sense of understanding and closure. But I feel numb, and I am completely devastated. I feel like a fool. How could I not see? How do I fight this very spiritual battle? I need to remember that God is the One who will fight my battles. But how?"

"I am so tired I can't even think about this anymore. But sleep seems to elude me. I can't seem to stop thinking about the whole situation. I can't seem to shut my brain off and rest. Every time I turn around, I discover more hurtful truths. Lord, I need your help to respond properly. Help me let this pain go and move forward. My "birthday surprise" in March was learning that infidelity was the true reason my husband left me. When he walked out the door, he had said only

PUTTING IT ALL TOGETHER

that he "needed a break from the kids and me." But that was not the whole truth. I found out that during the last eight months he had lived with me, he had been communicating through Facebook with an old high school girlfriend."

These entries were written in March, but a month before in February, I was not doing well. At. All.

I was planning to kill myself.

In February, I didn't understand what was happening. I didn't know about the infidelity. All I had was his shallow explanation of needing a break. That didn't make sense to me, as I've explained in earlier chapters. We had so much good going on.

I wanted the questions, confusion, turmoil, and pain to end.

As I was thinking about the suicide method of using a gun versus pulling my car into the garage, I walked through the entranceway of my home and headed to the garage. I shouted to God in my mind, "God, help; I can't take this anymore; I just can't stand the constant pain. It is not that I can't live without my husband. It is just that the pain never seems to go away. It is like that constant 'drip, drip, drip' of rain on a tin roof—irritating, annoying, and a never-ending source of bewilderment." As I was walking towards the garage, I heard these words, so loud and crystal clear they stopped me dead in my tracks: *"Let this mind be in you, which was also in Christ Jesus"* and *"thou wilt keep him in perfect peace whose mind is stayed on thee."* (Philippians 2:5 and Isaiah 26:3a) I stopped, paused and looked around, trying to see who was speaking.

Comprehension dawned that the voice was in my head. I believe God spoke to me that day. Realization dawned on me: "Oh my goodness, that's it! That is what I am not doing. I am not letting God fill my mind because I am focusing on my pain."

I was like Peter who stepped out of the boat and looked around at the wind, rain, and the storm. When he looked around at the circumstances, he instantly began to sink (Matthew 14: 22-33)!

My focus was not on Jesus Christ but on my circumstances. Just like Peter, I was sinking in the storm when instead I should have been running for cover into my Savior's arms. And just like Peter, as he was sinking, He cried for Jesus to help, as did I. God put those thoughts in my head to help me realize this was a battle for my mind. He helped me see I had allowed the circumstances to dictate my thought life.

I knew the healing process had to include a change in my thinking. That day, one of the lowest, darkest days so far, became another turning point for me with my mindset, my focus. When I cried out "God help," He did, immediately! He spoke words of encouragement to ease my troubled mind. He was there like the Good Shephard guiding me back to Him. All I had to do was turn my eyes, look at Him, and believe He would take care of the storm.

Months earlier I had asked God to help me understand the way to ultimate healing. This fourth lesson God taught me was another foundational truth towards understanding full healing process. For me, this lesson was like the "cherry-on-top" or like the drawstring that pulled everything together, so I could finally obtain the healing for which I had been searching.

I want you to experience God's healing in the same way I did. I want us to stop walking around like the "walking wounded" and embrace the healing that comes from God when we completely surrender to Him.

Have you ever heard that saying that it gets worse before it gets better? That is what happened in my situation. In my life, before healing could begin, a thorough sifting needed to occur. You may find the same thing has to happen in your life too. Keep moving forward! You will find the healing you long for!

Peter's Sifting

The best example I can give to demonstrate this sifting I am referring to is to look at the life of Peter in Luke.

Some of us might be familiar with a well-known Scripture passage recounting a time when Peter walked on water, but I want to look at who Peter was as a man. I think many of us will find we can relate to Peter.

Peter was a fisherman by trade and seemed to have all the qualities of a leader yet in an unrefined way. He was the most outspoken of the disciples, forceful and restless at times, but extremely loyal. If he believed in something, you were not going to change his mind; he was resolute. He was the inquisitive one of the bunch, hardened by life yet in the end softened by the love of his friend and Savior,

Jesus. For these reasons I love Peter. In addition, he reminds me of myself in certain ways. I seem to open my mouth and insert my foot often, just like Peter. Can you relate to that?

If Peter was living today, I imagine he would be the kind of guy about which some might say, "I don't like him, but I admire his spunk." Then there would be others who would blindly follow him; he was just that kind of guy. He did everything in extremes, so when he stood up with and for Jesus people noticed.

Because of his loud and large personality, people also readily noticed when he messed up. We are going to look at a big failure in Peter's life. Like everything he did, he messed up well and good, from one extreme to the other. Those "mess-ups" created wounds in his soul from which he would need healing.

Jesus knew Peter was going to walk away from Him. In fact, Jesus tells him this after Peter announced, in a grand gesture, that he would follow Him to prison or death.

Luke 22:33-34, *"And he said unto him, 'Lord, I am ready to go with thee, both into prison, and to death.' And he said, 'I tell thee, Peter, the cock shall not crow this day, before that thou shalt thrice deny that thou knowest me.'"*

The verses that follow in Luke tell of Christ's agony at the crucifixion He was about to face. The story of Peter's betrayal continues in Luke 22: 54," *"Then took they him [Jesus], and led him, and brought him into the high priest's house. And Peter followed afar off."*

Putting It All Together

Just as Christ predicted, Peter denied Christ two times and immediately following the third denial, the Lord turned and looked at Peter. And Peter remembered the Word of the Lord, how He had said unto him, *"Before the cock crow, thou shalt deny me thrice.' And Peter went out and wept bitterly"* (Luke 22: 60-62).

Peter, who prided himself on being loyal and true, let his Friend down. I believe in Peter's mind he always thought he would have to physically fight a battle and that together, with Jesus at his side, they would win. Peter had never imagined this type of scenario. This was a serious, major denial of friendship. When his Friend, whom Peter promised to always stand beside, needed him the most, the urge to protect himself prevailed above friendship. Self-preservation kicked in. In one fell swoop, everything Peter prided himself in and believed in about himself was gone. He had done the unthinkable and turned his back on his best Friend. Peter, almost unable to live with what he had just done, went out and wept bitterly.

Then Peter turned back to the life he had lived as a fisherman before Jesus came into his life. In Peter's typical fashion, he threw himself "all in." Peter was once "all in" for Jesus but now, encased in hopelessness and despair, he left his calling of being a fisher of men to go back to the life of a fisherman. Going back to the life he once knew was easy to do, for there were no unknowns there. It seemed he was trying to forget.

Peter was wounded in a way that went deep into 'his soul. Let's remember the definition from Lesson One of a self-wound: an internal wound that causes a person to feel a negative emotion, such as hurt, bitterness, anger, rage, etc., which festers as time goes on.

Peter hated himself for what he had done, and all he could do was try to outrun the pain. This wound is one that many of us have probably experienced. We have all messed up royally and done some things we knew were absolutely wrong.

Let's look at this story from a different viewpoint, one that may cause you not to be so hard on Peter or on yourself. Let's put on those spiritual glasses we learned about in Lesson 3 and back up a verse. Let's see what was happening before Peter's grand announcement and subsequent events.

Here are the words Jesus said to Peter before he stated he would die for Him: *"And the Lord said, 'Simon, Simon, behold, Satan hath desired to have you, that he may sift you as wheat: But I have prayed for thee, that thy faith fail not: and when thou art converted, strengthen thy brethren'"* (Luke 22:31-32).

Goodness! Does reading that verse just open your eyes like it did mine to see what was really going on? Satan asked to put Peter through the proverbial ringer. God allowed it. Jesus prayed, interceding on Peter's behalf.

Peter's denial of Jesus created a soul wound. That wound was how Satan was able to get his foot in the door and attack Peter, putting him through the sieve. Again, soul wounds give the enemy a way to attack us, attempting to destroy us and our effectiveness by causing us to doubt our faith.

Sifted Like Wheat

Satan, Peter's enemy, wanted to squash Peter with the metal winnowing fork. Let me explain. The term "sifted like wheat" would have been understood in Jesus' time. When wheat is harvested, the kernel of wheat is encased inside the chaff, the dry covering around the grain. That dry covering is worthless, so it needs to be separated from the wheat. The wheat grain was beaten with a metal bar. Next, the farmer would take the wheat and pick it up with a winnowing fork which was used to loosen the grain of wheat from the chaff. As the farmer picked up the wheat, he would then toss it into the air. The wind would blow away the chaff, the unnecessary part from the wheat, leaving the wheat the farmer could grind up and make breads, pastries, and different types of food.

What I discovered is that while this process is difficult, it is necessary. Just as we can't eat or use the wheat as long as the chaff is still in the mix, Jesus might decide we need to go through this painful process. Jesus knew Peter had some pride in his life, some hard edges that needed to be softened. Jesus knew Peter could not be used to his full potential if the chaff was still encasing his life. Peter thought in his own strength and integrity he would protect Jesus. That was pride and it had to go.

I had some chaff in my life, too. God used a bad situation to "shift" the dry, dead, flaking chaff, so to speak, off my life.

I get a kick out of this next thought: Jesus used Satan to accomplish His purpose! Well, put that in your pipe and smoke it, right? What a concept! To be used by God, Peter needed to be rid of the chaff—his pride, his self-suffering, his depending on himself—to be gone. Jesus used Satan to accomplish His purposes, and He prayed that Peter's faith would not fail.

> Jesus used Satan to accomplish His purpose!

There is that word again, faith. Remember the lessons that came before this. Do you see how faith, soul wounds, and spiritual warfare are all interlinked? Peter's pride represents the chaff (the soul wounds), Satan creates spiritual warfare, and Peter's failure caused him to doubt his faith.

Do we do the same thing? Let's take some time to examine our lives right now. What area in your life represents the chaff? What area needs to be sifted?

Peter was called to tell others about Jesus. Just because he messed up did not mean God revoked His calling. God never takes back His gifts or His calling (Romans 8:29).

During separation or divorce, we might feel some of the same things Peter felt—shame, failure, tainted, not good enough.

Putting It All Together

We must stand firm in our faith, with the full armor of God protecting us, and wield our sword. Go back to review the truth of Ephesians 6:10-17.

Satan thought he scored another victory. But he didn't. God knows our soul wounds are like the chaff surrounding our hearts. Those wounds need to be sifted, shaken off, just like chaff on the wheat. That sifting is a necessary process to get to the "good stuff" so the "wheat" (our lives) can be used to advance the Kingdom of God. Just like Peter, you and I need healing and are going to be sifted. The choice is ours as to whether we allow that sifting to occur and let the chaff — soul wounds — fly away or stick to us. That sifting, if we allow it, will move along the healing process.

Before the sifting, before the healing, what do we know of Peter? We know he is boisterous, outgoing, a leader, and a follower of Jesus. Do we read of any major moments of impact on others before his "sifting"? I would argue that while he was one of the more dominant disciples, we didn't see him accomplishing much.

In John 21:13-19 we see Jesus came back to Peter for a one-on-one conversation. Jesus was giving Peter a second chance to do what He called Peter to do. Jesus was seeking to restore and draw Peter back to His inner fold.

Peter, loved and redeemed by Jesus Christ, had been sifted. Peter was changed — pride gone, now humbled and healed. He was able to then reach thousands who became followers of Jesus. Throughout the book of Acts, we see that through the disciples, the entire Roman

Empire heard the Gospel. Acts 17:6 b says they "turned the world upside down," *Strong's Concordance* says the word *world* references the "globe, specifically the Roman empire: earth world." Peter was a major contributor in that amazing feat. Can you imagine? Every single person who was alive during the end of the disciples' and Paul's ministry heard the gospel – without the help of the internet or Facebook! That took dedication and a whole, healed, pure heart.

At this point in my separation, I needed to know, systematically, how to be healed, just like Peter. That was my original prayer in the very beginning of the separation. Maybe it is the list maker in me or the business side of me that wanted "A Plan of Action for Success" that caused me to continue to ask God HOW to be healed, step by step. God is a God of order (1 Corinthians 14:40), and He says that if any man asks for wisdom, He will give it to him liberally (James 1:5). While the process was not always linear, God did reveal to me a systematic, orderly plan.

Four Steps Toward Healing

God revealed to me a plan that led me to healing. I encourage each of you to seek Jesus—seek Him with all your might.

Maybe you will find the same steps to healing. Maybe you will use some of the principles. Whatever course you take, just keep turning to Him and surrendering all to the Lord.

Below is the Four-Step Plan God gave me to neutralize soul wounds and heal from the inside out. They are…

- Acknowledge the pain
- Leave it at the cross
- Ask for healing
- Claim resurrection power

Step One: Acknowledge the Pain

Once we decide to allow the sifting to occur, to remove those old soul wounds (the chaff), the first step in the healing process of our journey can begin. Whether the journey is to heal small or large wounds, we follow the same steps. Getting rid of or letting go of the chaff (soul wounds) can be hard, painful, but utterly necessary if we want a heart made whole.

The healing journey begins by acknowledging the pain we feel. Or if you committed a sin, the first step is to openly and honestly admit that sin. NO SUGAR COATING.

I am going to walk you through what that looked like for me. I am going to let you be the proverbial "fly on the wall." Ok, are you ready? No judging, please.

I would get in my prayer room and I spoke OUT LOUD to God, as I would to a physical person I could see. He is, after all, my best friend, it was time I stopped just saying He was my friend and started acting like it.

The conversation sounded something like this: "God, right now, I am so mad I could spit! I am so hurt it feels like a knife is sticking straight in my heart, and my husband is turning it around and around. I gave him everything, and in return, he betrayed me. God, this hurts so, so very much. At times, I feel so enraged I now understand the woman who made the name "Bobbitt" a household name. I totally understand the raw emotions that land others in jail for doing something outrageous in the heat of the moment. I want to swear a blue streak up and down. God, I know you know what swear words I want to use right now, but I am going to refrain! What happened was so wrong, and it is so deeply painful."

A little out there, right? Why do we think that when we pray to God, we have to come in a pious, holier-than-thou and self-righteous way? God knows my every thought. He knows yours. Not speaking our true thoughts when we speak to Him only hurts us. He did not tell us to pray because He didn't know what we were thinking. He told us to pray because prayer is for us. We are the ones who need to admit what we think and feel. That is why God gives us a phenomenal principle in John 8:32 which says, *"And ye shall know the truth and the truth shall make you free."* We need to know the truth, and with that truth firmly in our minds, freedom *will* follow. Verse 34b continues with the thought and explains further, *"Whosoever committeth sin is the servant of sin."* All those raw emotions, if left unchecked turn to sin. I did not want to be a servant of sin.

Acknowledging and then admitting those feelings are very powerful steps. In order for full healing to occur, we can't stop with the first step of acknowledging and admitting. To see the healing process come to fruition, we must follow the rest of the steps.

Step Two: Leave it at the Foot of the Cross

Once those emotions are laid bare, we can then take them to the foot of the cross. The Scripture is clear that the blood atones (cancels out) the sins (wounds) in our souls. Here are just a few verses:

Leviticus 17:11b, *"...it is the blood that maketh an atonement for the soul."*

Hebrews 9:22b, *"...and without shedding of blood is no remission [forgiveness]."*

1 John 1:7b-10, *"...and the blood of Jesus Christ his Son cleanseth us from all sin. If we say that we have no sin, we deceive ourselves, and the truth is not in us. If we confess our sins, he is faithful and just to forgive us our sins, and to cleanse us from all unrighteousness. If we say that we have not sinned, we make him a liar, and his word is not in us."*

When we commit a sin, Satan accuses us in the courtroom of heaven, we are found guilty (*There is none righteous, no not one. Romans 3:10*), judgement is rendered, but instead of paying the penalty, when we seek God's forgiveness, Jesus steps in and presents the blood that He shed on the cross, He takes the punishment (*For the wages of sin is death...Romans 6:23a*) on Himself for us (*For he [Jesus] hath made him to be sin for us, who knew no sin; that we might be made the righteousness of God in him. 2 Corinthians 5:21*), we accept that forgiveness and take the gift of his sacrifice (*but the gift of God is eternal life through Jesus Christ our Lord Romans 6:23b*) the penalty was paid. All we have to do is ask for His punishment to be applied as payment for our debt. Then our sins are gone. We can never be charged on that specific offence again. Praise the Lord!

I would take time out to enter a quiet place where I lay all these issues out before the Lord. I prayed that God would reveal any hurts, bitterness, or anger, any sin in my life that still needed to be acknowledged and then confessed. I would continue in prayer, getting all my emotions, feelings, and thoughts out until there was nothing left to say about that particular situation. I would just keep talking, out loud, until I took a deep breath and then heaved a large sigh of relief. I knew all those negative emotions were laid out on the table so to speak. I was being honest with myself. At times, that is so hard to do. Self-deception is one way Satan tricks us into thinking we are okay. It is a powerful tool in his toolbox. I didn't want to allow anything to hinder my healing, so honesty was a must!

Once I felt that release, I would move on. I knelt in prayer, and while kneeling, I pictured Jesus on the cross. With my arms extended, as if all those words I had just spoken were in my hands, I laid them down at the foot of Jesus. I asked Jesus Christ to take my pain, my sorrow, my hurt, my rejection, and my sin. I asked Him to forgive me for my bitterness and asked Him to help me forgive.

That was a very tough thing to say. And it wasn't until I really started to try and forgive those hurts that my own path to healing began. Remember this method applies if we have been sinned against. The initial offence is painful, and it hurts. Those wounds we have received, when left to fester, can turn into sin, i.e. bitterness, anger, resentment. Once I understood I had to deal with an offence right away, I could still use this same scenario to seek healing from wounds others inflicted on me. I did not want any initial hurts to turn into sin, so I was able to quickly deal with offences and move on.

A reminder about forgiveness: Forgiving doesn't necessarily mean you just ignore bad behavior or avoid seeking true justice from the appropriate legal or spiritual authorities (depending on the situation). It doesn't mean you condone bad behavior. It just means you are letting go, turning the hurt and pain over to the Lord, so healing can take place.

I wanted my sins to be as far as is the east is from the west, never to be remembered, as Psalm 103:12 tells us, *"As far as the east is from the west, so far hath he removed our transgressions [sin] from us."* The significance referencing the east and west is the fact those two points *never* meet. Those sins can never come before God again, even if the enemy or we try to bring those sins up again. Our sins are gone—forever!

Step Three: Ask for Healing

How can we receive healing? The Bible promises healing from two sources. One is through The Word of God and the other is under the protection of His wings.

We find this promise in Psalm 91:4, *"He shall cover thee with his feathers, and under his wings shalt thou trust: his truth shall be thy shield and buckler. Then they cry unto the LORD in their trouble, and he saveth them out of their distresses.* ***He sent his word, and healed them, and delivered them from their destructions."***

In the book of Psalms, I found my words, my strength, and my ability to continue the healing process. Using the words from these Scriptures, I would pray, asking God to take care of my enemies or family members who were attacking my character. I would ask Him to hear me and heal me. Psalm 143 and Psalm 18 were favorites, and they would be great Scriptures for you to look up and incorporate in your prayers. I prayed that God would be my shield and buckler. He would be my refuge. He would be my high tower. He would confound them that were coming after me. Every single time I did that, God gave me a victory.

Putting It All Together

Attacks from the enemy came to my mind, and they were constant, hard and fast with no relief in sight. Most of my attacks were in the form of little negative voices in my head. Dianna Kokoszka, a trainer for BOLD with Keller Williams Realty, refers to those negative voices in our heads as "drunk monkeys." I like that word picture. Think about it, when someone is drunk, even though they may say funny things, you probably wouldn't take their advice, right? Their words are not based on good, sound judgement because their mind is impaired. The same is true with those "drunk monkeys" coming at you in your mind, maybe even right now. Our emotions and thoughts are impaired due to the trauma or wounds that have been inflicted on us and it is hard to think properly.

So, I would constantly remind myself that my fight was not against flesh and blood but against "spiritual wickedness" and demonic influences coming against me trying to steal my faith, trying to make me cave, give in, go away, and stop standing! When those moments would occur, I prayed that God would be my protector.

I prayed that I would *"find favor with God and man,"* and I specifically asked God to show me favor as He did within the life of Jesus (Luke 2:52). *Strong's Concordance* defines favor as "the divine influence upon the heart...and life, benefit, gift, grace, joy, pleasure." I wanted that favor just as Jesus Christ received it from God the Father.

For several weeks I was daily repeating this phrase in prayer, I was getting ready to go to court. I hated the fact that I was going to court against my husband. My attorney suggested I file a Temporary Restraining Order (TRO) on him because he sold a third of our business without consulting me. I didn't know what to do, so I just kept praying and crying out to God. I loved my husband and didn't care about the money, although I desperately needed it. I turned the situation over to God and emailed the attorneys on both sides, saying I wanted to withdraw. Whatever my husband decided to do was fine with me. My attorney and my counselor both had a fit!

Apparently, I was thinking with my imbalanced emotions. The best advice I got that day was from my Christian counselor who gently reminded me that the state of North Carolina has already decided a 50/50 split was the way it should be and was fair to both parties. She felt that allowing him to decide about the money was to condone his behavior of adultery and abandonment. To give in was sending a message that it was okay to walk away from his vows and that there would be no consequences.

Once I decided to listen to the counsel around me, I moved forward with the TRO. I needed to go to court. I prayed again that I would "find favor with God and with man," and whatever was right and just that God would move in the heart of the judge. I was amazed at the outcome. The judge ruled in my favor. We had to go back a second time, and that time my husband was found in contempt of court because he failed to obey the ruling. Two times I had

Putting It All Together

to go into the courtroom against my will. Yet each time I believe I found favor with God and with man. It was another testament of God's love being displayed in a real physical way. It gave me the mental strength to get through another day. When I was able to claim the Word of God and stand on His promises the shattered places in my heart began to heal. I began to believe again that God truly cared about every part of me.

Sometimes God's answer to my prayer was something small, such as a song coming on the radio that would answer a question I had or a Scripture verse that was sent by a friend. For a while, God's response came through numbers. If you do a quick look up on the internet for "Biblical Numerology" you will find a chart that shows the significance of certain numbers as related to the Bible. I kept seeing the number 5, specifically on a clock. For instance, the number 5 represents grace, so 5:55 on the clock was a reminder that God's grace would get me through with His abundant grace. 2 Corinthians 4:14-15 uses the words abundant grace. *Strong's Concordance* defines abundant as "to do, make, or be more that is increase; to super abound." Grace refers to God's graciousness or influence on the heart and life and it is an "acceptable benefit, favor, gift, or pleasure." Reminders of God's grace, which causes us "not to faint" but to be "renewed," according to 2 Corinthians 4:16, was the encouraging boost I needed.

Other times, God would show me favor in a greater way. I will never forget a time when I prayed for favor during a particularly challenging mental battle. I needed to know that God cared! I needed to know the battle was being won, that the victory for my mind was in sight. The clanging sounds from the symbols of defeat were ringing loud in my ear, and I didn't know how much more I could take.

I marched myself down to the mailbox to get my mail. I found "real" mail which was a nice surprise, not the junk mail or the pre-stamped marketing pieces we are so accustomed to seeing. It was a letter from a past client when my husband and I were still together. She was a sweetheart and dear to both of us. In that letter, I found a check with my name on it. Now that is not the amazing part. The amazing part was that the amount of the check was left BLANK! I was so startled I dropped the check like it was a hot potato. Who does that?

Here is what I thought was especially amazing. I had prayed for favor two days before. That means God was already lining up a "kiss from God." God knew what I was going to need. At just the right time, God had put into the heart of a wonderful lady to send that blank check to bless me in an amazing way. Do you know what amount I put on that check? $5.55, the numbers symbolizing God's grace.

I laminated a copy of that check and use it as a bookmark in my Bible as a reminder of God's love. Isn't God so very good?

Over that year, I would type or write out promises found in the Bible, specifically in the book of Psalms. There was no rhythm or rhyme, just whatever I needed for that moment. I would write out verses and claim them. Every time I claimed a promise, I would receive a victory. Maybe not the exact way I wanted physically, but spiritually. I was growing and healing – just as His Word promised.

So many times, during my own trial, I would think of a storm and feel once again like Peter when he stepped out of the boat. I was drowning in the storms of life. At times, I would immediately remember, and other times it would take me a while, that I would sink if my focus was on the storm instead of on God and His promises. As I refocused my mind on Jesus Christ, then He would bring to my remembrance a song or a passage of Scripture like the ones below. I was often drawn to Scriptures referring to wings of protection.

One day as I was praying one of these Scriptures, I stopped and asked God why He used wings to demonstrate His protection and a place to be healed. Think about it: have you ever seen a duck in a pond come out of the water looking like a drowned rat? No, God created them with the ability to make their feathers waterproof with their preen gland and a powder their feathers create.

While camping or sitting in a park, I often watched the local ducks and their ducklings as they swam. The adult ducks bobbed their heads down into the water to catch a little snack. When they'd lift their heads, the water would just kind of slide right off their feathers. It's amazing they did not get waterlogged.

Now baby ducks are a different story, as they do not yet have fully waterproofed feathers. When a storm comes, they must seek shelter under their mother's wings. Their little legs cause them to look like drunken sailors as they wobble towards shelter. Their mother tucks them up and under her wings. I can just see them now as they run head first under her wings, burying their heads to block out the storm, waiting for their fear and the rain to subside! Then as time passes and the storm begins to lessen, they peek their heads out. As the storm abates, and they feel brave enough, they venture out of that safe place, at first tentatively then with more confidence.

When I feel I am in the middle of life's storm, I think of those ducks' wings. If they were big enough when rain started pouring down, they would make an awesome place to run and hide! Unlike an umbrella which only gives a head covering, under those wings, we would be dry and warm as we would be fully enveloped to ward off the wind-whipping rain drops.

Jesus is to us what a momma duck is to her ducklings. We have been offered large wings to which we can run and take shelter under. Let's read some verses with that picture in mind. We have a place that is safe, dry, and warm. We have a shelter to rest in until the storm passes by. Our only responsibility is to get there, to seek, and to follow hard after God.

Psalm 63: 7-8, *"Because thou hast been my help, therefore in the shadow of thy wings will I rejoice. My soul followeth hard after thee: thy right hand upholdeth me."*

Psalm 91: 4, *"He shall cover thee with his feathers, and under his wings shalt thou trust: his truth shall be thy shield and buckler."*

Psalm 57: 1-2, *"Be merciful unto me, O God, be merciful unto me: for my soul trusteth in thee: yea, in the shadow of thy wings will I make my refuge, until these calamities be overpast. I will cry unto God most high; unto God that performeth all things for me."*

How amazing is our God? He gives us word pictures so we might actually feel like we are climbing under His wings where He is going to wrap us up in His protection and love. In the shelter of His wings, we can receive the healing we so desperately need. Snuggled up in His arms is an amazing place to be. I found that place when I set aside a quiet place to read and pray. Other times I felt I was under His wings watching events play out where He was doing something special…just for me.

I think God brings storms into our lives for a purpose. Storms in our lives can cause us to turn away from God in discouragement and bitterness or the storms of separation or divorce can lead us to keep God as the center of our existence which gives us stability. As we are resting in Him waiting for the storm to pass, if we seek refuge in Him, we can continue the healing process through the Word of God.

Below are three more verses that promise healing through the Word of God. These are great Scriptures to write out. Place them on your refrigerator or bathroom mirror. Use them as a reminder that you can receive healing and where it comes from.

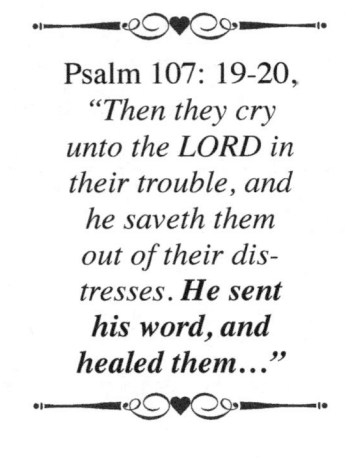

Psalm 107: 19-20, *"Then they cry unto the LORD in their trouble, and he saveth them out of their distresses.* **He sent his word, and healed them..."**

Psalm 119: 49-50, *"Remember the word unto thy servant, upon which thou hast caused me to hope. This is my comfort in my affliction:* **for thy word hath quickened me.***"*

So many times over the past year the feeling of brokenness lingered inside me until I pulled the Word of God out, read His promises, claimed them, and was rejuvenated. God's Word saved me from a life of despondency, rejection, and despair. Only through winding the Word of God tightly in our minds are we able to be saved and lifted out of the pit of pain.

God knows our thoughts. Isaiah 9:6 says He is our Counselor. He is our Advisor, and He knows us intimately. His Word will pierce into our hearts with exactly what we need at just the perfect moment. When we pick up the only offensive weapon we have, the Word of God, and use it, then and only then will we win. No team or army ever succeeded or won a battle by only playing defense. In order to stand in victory, we must use the Sword of the Lord which is the Word of God.

Putting It All Together

*"For the word of God is quick, and powerful, and sharper than any two-edged sword, **piercing** even to the dividing asunder of **soul and spirit**, and of the joints and marrow, and is a discerner of the thoughts and intents of the heart."* Hebrews 4:12

As I hear God's Word, either through reading or listening online, or as I heard music and sermons, the Holy Spirit was soothing my soul by bringing to remembrance promises from the Scriptures I could claim and wave high in the air when doubt started to creep in. The Holy Spirit would give me wisdom, a gentle nudge, or a nugget of knowledge I desperately needed at the precise moment. He was leading and guiding me. It was comforting. It was healing.

Those moments are hugs and kisses from our Heavenly Father. They are everywhere; we just have to watch out for them. Those moments bring healing to our wounded souls, as we cling to the promises found in the Scriptures and then see them coming to fruition.

Step Four: Claim the Power of the Resurrection

Like me, you may have heard phrases such as the following without fully grasping their meaning:

"The power is in the blood."
"The power is in the cross."
"The power is in the resurrection."

When I asked God to show me how to heal, He drew my attention to these phrases. I needed to learn what this "power" was that we are supposed to have as children of God. I decided to do some research on the word "power" and all the verses that word was used. What I discovered was so profound it changed my life.

Through the power of the cross, we can overcome. The cross is where we get our strength and power. As we've learned previously, this word "power" is the Greek word *dunamis* which means "force (literally or figuratively); **miraculous power**, **might** (-y, deed), **(worker of) miracles**, power, strength, **mighty (wonderful) work**" (*Strong's*).

Note the word **power** in the following verses:

Philippians 3:10a, *"That I may know him, and the **power** of his resurrection."*

I Corinthians 6:14, *"And God hath both raised up the Lord, and will also raise up us **by his own power**."*

Jesus gained this power when He went through the process of dying, being buried in the grave, and on the third day rising from the dead. When Jesus Christ overcame the grave, He earned the right to "spoil" or disarm the enemy: *"And you, being dead in your sins and the uncircumcision of your flesh, hath he quickened together with him, having forgiven you all trespasses; Blotting out*

Putting It All Together

the handwriting of ordinances that was against us, which was contrary to us, and took it out of the way, nailing it to his cross; And having spoiled principalities and powers, he made a shew of them openly, triumphing over them in it" (Colossians 2:13-15).

Let me put the above verses into perspective. In the days of the Bible, a common practice whenever a victory occurred was to strip off the enemies' clothes and then to chain the soldiers together with their commander in front. Next, the victorious would parade them around the city streets proclaiming they won the battle. It was their way of demonstrating the enemy had been conquered. When the citizens saw the enemy being paraded in chains, they had a sense of peace and power knowing these enemies could never hurt them again. Just as they openly paraded and proclaimed freedom from the tyrants of that day, we as Christians have the same power against the spiritual enemies.

That same power in Jesus Christ is given to each one of us; it is our inheritance! Read the promise below, claim it as your own.

*"That the God of our Lord Jesus Christ, the Father of glory, may give unto you the spirit of wisdom and revelation in the knowledge of him: The eyes of your understanding being enlightened; that ye may know what is the hope of his calling, and **what the riches of the glory of his inheritance in the saints**, And **what is the exceeding greatness of his power to us-ward who believe**, according to the working of **his mighty power**, Which he wrought in Christ, when*

he raised him from the dead, and set him at his own right hand in the heavenly places," (Ephesians 1:18-20).

Acts 26:18 also references our inheritance - our right to claim the power of Jesus Christ. When we turn to Jesus Christ and accept Him as Lord of our life, we are filled with the Holy Spirit which gives us the same power to overcome and stop the wounds from taking over our lives. The healing and rebuilding can begin anew.

Jeremy Camps song, "Same Power," has captured exactly what we need to remember about our inheritance of power. The Holy Spirit rose Jesus Christ from the grave and He now lives in us.

This was one of my go-to songs. It was on my playlist, and I listened to it almost daily for three months straight. I needed to be reminded that the same power that raised Jesus Christ from the dead lives in me. When we accept the gift of salvation Jesus offers us, we receive the power of God. It transforms our lives. It gives us strength deep within us, in our "inner man" which is our soul, it has the power to heal. As you read these next few verses, watch for the use of the word power—*dunamis* power—a miraculous, strong, mighty force.

Romans 1:16a, *"For I am not ashamed of the gospel of Christ: for it is the power of God unto salvation to every one that believeth."*

Putting It All Together

Ephesians 3:16, *"That he would grant you, according to the riches of his glory, to be strengthened with might [or dunamis/power] by his Spirit in the inner man."*

Ephesians 3:20, *"Now unto him that is able to do exceeding abundantly above all that we ask or think, according to the power that worketh in us."*

2 Corinthians 13: 4-5, *"For though he was crucified through weakness, yet he liveth by the power of God. For we also are weak in him, but we shall live with him by the power of God toward you. Examine yourselves, whether ye be in the faith; prove your own selves."*

I had to keep reminding myself of what we discussed in Lesson 2—the power of faith. Faith has the POWER to save, to heal, and to move mountains. That is powerful. That is amazing. That is miraculous! Why does faith have that power? Because of the cross. This power of faith through and because of Jesus Christ is our inheritance to carry us successfully through life. Claim your inheritance. The only time we are not living a victorious, holy life is any time we are not claiming the power. I challenge you--the next time you read through the New Testament, watch how the disciples claimed that power. They commanded demons to leave the possessed, they spoke healing into the lives of the sick, and they shared that faith to save the lost. We can too. Pretty amazing!

Healing Is Like Peeling an Onion

As we close this chapter about the healing process, again I want to remind you the healing process is not necessarily a linear, step-by-step process.

I used to get discouraged thinking I had been completely healed, but then a memory would trigger a spiral down the ladder of despair. I felt like I was on a crazy roller coaster ride.

When my good friend and mentor, Linda, explained that our wounds are deep, and they are much like layers of an onion, I stopped being so hard on myself. Sometimes we receive healing from a soul wound all at one time, but other times, like the peeling of an onion, we peel off one layer of that soul wound at a time. That is why we can continue to struggle. Our enemy is tricky and will keep using the same old tired lines. Then one day we smarten up and learn his tricks. When that happens, he will change his tactics and throw us a curve ball. It can knock us down, and as we land hard on our bottoms, we can either laugh or cry, but we must decide if we are going to stay down or ask God for the strength to get back up.

I hope you've seen throughout the lessons of this book so far that turning to God is a constant choice we make day by day and moment by moment.

Putting It All Together

To reach complete healing became my choice, and it becomes yours, too. If we want to live a healthy, whole life, we must apply the steps toward healing by acknowledging the pain, leaving it at the cross, asking for healing, and claiming the resurrection power. These are keys that will open the door to a healthy soul

> Healing became my choice, and it becomes yours, too.

Healing Tools

Memorize Scripture: *"...he hath sent me (Jesus) to bind up the brokenhearted, to proclaim liberty to the captives, and the opening of the prison to them that are bound; To proclaim the acceptable year of the LORD, and the day of vengeance of our God; to comfort all that mourn; To appoint unto them that mourn in Zion, to give unto them beauty for ashes, the oil of joy for mourning, the garment of praise for the spirit of heaviness; that they might be called trees of righteousness, the planting of the LORD, that he might be glorified"* (Isaiah 61:1b-3)

Meditate on the Journal of Psalms: *"Be merciful unto me, O God, be merciful unto me: for my soul trusteth in thee: yea, in the shadow of thy wings will I make my refuge, until these calamities be overpast. I will cry unto God most high; unto God that performeth all things for me"* (Psalm 57:1-2).

Shattered Souls Made Whole

"Because thou hast been my help, therefore in the shadow of thy wings will I rejoice. My soul followeth hard after thee: thy right hand upholdeth me" (Psalm 63:7-8).

"He shall cover thee with his feathers, and under his wings shalt thou trust: his truth shall be thy shield and buckler. Then they cry unto the LORD in their trouble, and he saveth them out of their distresses. He sent his word, and healed them, and delivered them from their destructions" (Psalm 91:4).

Praise Daily and Often: Lord, I will praise You for being my refuge, my shelter in the storm. I thank You that I can find healing in Your Word. You are an amazing God!

Prayer Decree: God, be merciful to me when I am weak and forget to run to You. Let my soul search You out, to follow hard after You. Help me remember the Word of God is my source of healing and there is safety in your arms.

Focused Thought: Jesus was sent to turn our ashes into beauty, our mourning into joy, and our heavy shattered souls into praise filled hearts.

Lesson 5

Power of Effective Prayer

My Journal: February 3

"I have just gone through a seriously bad, very depressing weekend and cried buckets of tears. Those salty teardrops came hard and fast, streaming down my face like bitter rivers. I believe I am grieving the death of my marriage because my husband still intends to file divorce papers. My tears are not because I can't live without him. I just can't stand the constant pain, that awful feeling that never seems to go away, the agony of rejection, the silence, the feeling like a failure as a mother and wife, being at home by myself for days! I have thought about the possibility of giving up my dog. I have been thinking about the upcoming move out of the office I shared with my husband. And the pain of loss is a double-whammy because he was not only my husband but also my best friend. In a little over sixty days, I've lost so much. I even feel I've lost my own children, in a way. The weight of depression sits on me. Some days, I manage to overcome the feelings, but on days like today, they seem to swallow me up and engulf me. God, does it even matter if

I pray anymore? It doesn't seem to help. No matter how much I cry out to You, nothing changes. The situation stays the same. Does prayer really change things?"

※

Have you ever wondered if your prayers are being heard? Does God really listen, or do you feel like your pleas and petitions are just bouncing off the ceiling? Does prayer even matter? If you've had these thoughts, you're not alone. I'd venture to say all Christians have felt this way at some point. When it feels like you are alone in the dark, when you feel like you have no recourse, that's when you need to know how to pray effectively, more than ever; at least for me this is true.

In the very beginning of the separation, in those deep heart-wrenching moments, I had no words. I could not have prayed a thing if my life had depended on it. There was so much pain I didn't even know where to begin. I couldn't think or process much. I would just cling to the promise in Romans 8:26 that *"the Spirit itself maketh intercession for us with groanings which cannot be uttered."* The Holy Spirit was interceding on my behalf, and I needed to be okay with that during the time of shock and grief. If that is where you are right now, that is okay. The words will come, but for now, rest in His grace and ask Him to fill your heart and mind with words He speaks. His grace will get you through.

In my darkest times, when I found my words again, I prayed, read my Bible, and asked God for answers. God reminded me of a promise from James 5:16. *"The effectual fervent prayer of a righteous man availeth much."* This is a promise, but I had to ask God to help me truly understand it. I poured my heart out to my God, my Friend, and I read His Word, looking for answers.

The Bible says to compare Scripture with Scripture, so I began searching for more understanding of effective prayer. I was reminded of God's promises as I read further in James chapter 5:

Is any among you afflicted? Let him pray. Is any merry? Let him sing psalms. Is any sick among you? Let him call for the elders of the church; and let them pray over him, anointing him with oil in the name of the Lord: And the prayer of faith shall save the sick, and the Lord shall raise him up; and if he has committed sins, they shall be forgiven him. Confess your faults one to another, and pray one for another, that ye may be healed. The effectual fervent prayer of a righteous man availeth much (James 5:13-16).

I was sick, sick of the heartache and I wanted healing—healing for my children and myself. I wanted to know that God was hearing my cries.

Prayer Is the Moving Force of Change

When I asked God if prayer changes things, it was really my faith that was being tested, not God's ability to answer my prayers. That sneaky enemy Satan was attempting to strip and destroy my faith in the one true God who makes the impossible possible…again. My depression was proof the enemy did not want me to find those answers. Why? Because Satan knows that *the prayer of faith shall save the sick*. This is a powerful concept. Broken hearts need the healing power that prayer brings. The fact that our prayers have the power to bring healing from illness and disease of the mind, body, and soul is life-altering.

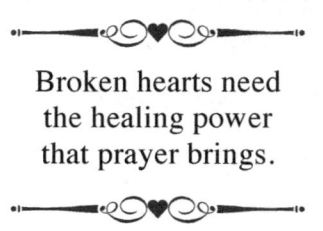

> Broken hearts need the healing power that prayer brings.

Even while my faith was tested, that same God, my God, mentioned by David in Psalm 145:8-9, continued with His graciousness, granting me His tender mercies and compassion that I sorely needed. Knowing I was truly seeking answers, God presented relevant Scriptures to my mind and provided what I so desperately needed at that time.

When we are going through a separation or a divorce, we **daily** have unanswered questions and concerns about which approach to use with our spouse or ex-spouse, how to handle the needs of the children, where to live, where to move, what to say to our in-laws or other family members. It is a constant, daily challenge. Knowing we are hearing from God and walking down the path He knows is best is one of the hardest things we will do. Listening and hearing the whispered words of God, so we know exactly where to turn, is an art form that takes practice to get right every time. Yet God has compassion on us and even when we don't "get it right" the first time, He does answer our prayers.

Let me tell of a time when a woman's prayer was answered, as clear as if a neon flashing sign hung in the sky.

My stomach was in knots, I was indecisive and completely at a loss on what to do. My husband and I had split up for numerous reasons, and I was torn. It was close to Mother's Day, and my heart was breaking for my children. I wanted to do the right thing, but I didn't know what that was with all the conflicting facts. One minute my husband expressed a desire to get back together and the next he was spending an inordinately unusual amount of time with another woman. He strongly insisted the relationship was purely a friendship.

I was trudging along in the aisles of Walmart with all those conflicting thoughts running through my head. I was weighing the pros and cons and asking myself questions such as:

"Do we get back together or not?"
"Can I believe what he says or is he lying."
"Does he just want to keep up appearances so he can continue to stay as head Pastor?"
"Should I stay for the children or stop the cycle of abuse?"

All these questions and more ran through my mind in rapid fire. As Mother's Day was fast approaching, I selected the cards for the mothers in my life and headed to the front of the store. As I wearily walked to the register, I began to cry out to God. "God, I need help. I do not know what to do. Should we reconcile or continue on this path of divorce?" I reached the register and laid the cards on the conveyor belt as I waited for my turn to check out. I glanced up, in the middle of my prayers, to see my husband walking into the store with a look of intimacy in his eye as he stared into the eyes of the woman on his arm. Swoosh! All the air in my lungs came out - as if I was sucker punched!

I guess I had my answer. "Thank You, God, for giving me clarity and answering all my questions in a blink of an eye. That was exactly what I needed to see as confirmation. Give me the strength to move forward."

Here was a woman who wanted to do things God's way, but there was no book in the Bible with verse and chapter she could turn to for the exact answer in this exact situation. That is the hard part about faith and knowing when God is actually answering our questions. In this situation, when she asked for clarity, God undeniably gave her the answer she needed.

So how do we individually know how to pray for our particular situation so our prayers are answered?

Breaking It Down: The Five A's of Prayer

In my search for answers on how to know if God was hearing my prayers, I went back to the basics and dug into the Word for guiding principles. I wanted to know my prayers would, in fact, be heard. In Matthew 6:9-13, Jesus demonstrates for us the pattern for praying: *"'After this manner therefore pray ye: Our Father which art in heaven, Hallowed be thy name. Thy kingdom come, Thy will be done in earth, as it is in heaven. Give us this day our daily bread. And forgive us our debts, as we forgive our debtors. And lead us not into temptation, but deliver us from evil: For thine is the kingdom, and the power, and the glory, forever.'"*

To help myself remember the pattern for prayer I came up with the five A's of prayer:

- **Acknowledge** the One I'm addressing (*Our Father which art in heaven, hallowed by thy name.*)
- **Align** my will with His, recognizing His dominion (*Thy Kingdom come, Thy will be done in Earth, as it is in Heaven.*)
- **Ask** for daily needs. (*Give us this day our daily bread.*)
- **Allow** Him to search my heart for any unforgiveness and then repent. (*Forgive us our debts, as we forgive our debtors.*)
- **Accept** that evil is out there and that we are all tempted to follow it. (*And lead us not into temptation, but deliver us from evil [from the evil one]*).

The book of Matthew gave me prayer principles, but I still needed the assurance that my prayers were not just flying around in space or hovering under my bedroom ceiling, unheard and wasted. So I dug deeper still. As I searched the Scriptures, I found the keys to knowing, beyond a shadow of a doubt, that God hears me. Whenever I questioned God about whether or not He was listening to me, He sent another verse into my path to enlighten me.

---

5 A's of prayer
Acknowledge
Align
Ask
Allow
Accept

The Effective Prayer of a Righteous Man

As I was on the path to understanding if my prayers were really being heard, I reread this verse in James 5:16b, *"The effectual fervent prayer of a righteous man availeth much."* After reading that verse again, slower this time, numerous questions popped into my mind. Who is a righteous man? Are my prayers effectual and fervent? Exactly how do my prayers avail anyway?

I dug deeply into the meaning of each main word in James 5:16b, bear with me as I break it down starting with the words *effectual* and *fervent*. According to *Strong's Concordance*, those two words were linked together from the Greek word *Energeo*, and I delved into its meaning along with the root words. Here are the multiple definitions of the words effective, fervent:

- be active, efficient, be mighty in

- (fixed) position (in place, time or state), and is the instrumentality
- it gives the understanding of working; to toil, an act

Hang in there; I know this is a lot of information to take in, but I will put it all back together in a minute. As for the righteous man, *Strong's Concordance* defines righteousness as "innocent." When we accept the free gift of salvation from Jesus, we are declared innocent or righteous as we stand before the throne of God. Our greatest attempt at righteousness is still like standing in filthy, dirty clothes when compared to that of Christ; the only righteousness we have is in Him. We can only stand in righteousness because of His blood, which covers our sins and saves us from being separated eternally from God. In Jesus, and with Him at our side, we can stand whole, sin-free, and forgiven. Jesus Christ serves as our Mediator, so we can pray with confidence if we have asked Him to forgive our sins and to be our Savior.

In the Greek, *availeth* means "to have (or exercise) force (literally or figuratively)" (*Strong's*). In other words, a righteous man's prayer has force behind it, and it is not meaningless. I don't know about you, but that excites me, to know my prayers are not just to hear myself talk but that they are for a purpose. Those prayers, muttered by little ol' me, have a force to move the spiritual realm, which affects the physical realm.

So with the definitions of the major words from James 5:16b listed above, we have a richer understanding of that verse. Let me put the verse back together. My active, working, operational prayers, spoken with passion, have a force behind them that are instrumental in bringing change, as I continually work (pray) from the fixed position as an innocent child of God. My prayers are powerful! If you are God's child, then your prayers are powerful. I now understand this quote from Martin Luther: "Work, work, from morning until late at night. In fact, I have so much to do that I shall have to spend the first three hours in prayer."

Prayer is the vehicle that enacts our faith, and God says, *"without faith it is impossible to please him: for he that cometh to God must believe that he is, and that he is a rewarder of them that diligently seek him"* (Hebrews 11:6). An effectual, fervent, praying person knows faith moves mountains, saves us, and heals us. This is a belief we can fashion after the Son Himself: *"Jesus answering saith unto them, 'Have faith in God. For verily I say unto you, that whosoever shall say unto this mountain, Be thou removed, and be thou cast into the sea; and shall not doubt in his heart, but shall believe that those things which he saith shall come to pass; he shall have whatsoever he saith'"* (Mark 11:22-23).

In Psalm 141:2 and Revelation 8:4 we see that our prayers are described as incense rising up to throne of God. That's a beautiful image to keep in mind as we pray.

I knew from different Scriptures that praying can bring a positive outcome to a negative situation, but in the recesses of my mind, I also remembered my prayers could be blocked or hindered.

Three Things That Block Our Prayers

I continued to sift through the Scriptures looking for all the things that can block the effectiveness of our prayer. I wanted to know both sides of the coin: how prayers are blocked and how to ensure the effectiveness of our prayers. First, let's look at certain actions that block our prayers.

#1 Prayer Blocker: Unforgiveness

"And when ye stand praying, forgive, if ye have fought against any: that your Father also which is in heaven may forgive you your trespasses. But if ye do not forgive, neither will your Father which is in heaven forgive your trespasses" (Mark 11:25-26).

#2 Prayer Blocker: Being Dishonoring or Disrespectful

"Likewise, ye husbands, dwell with them according to knowledge, giving honor unto the wife, as unto the weaker vessel, and as being heirs together of the grace of life; that your prayers be not hindered" (1 Peter 3:7).

#3 Prayer Blocker: Being Unwilling to Reconcile

"Therefore if thou bring thy gift to the altar, and there rememberest that thy brother hath ought against thee; leave there thy gift before the altar, and go thy way; first be reconciled to thy brother, and then come and offer thy gift" (Matthew 5:23-24).

One thing I want more than anything is the assurance that when I pray, God hears me. This may sound selfish, but one day as I was studying the verses on what blocks my prayers, one of my children needed help that could only come from God. I went to the Lord in prayer, but first I examined myself and asked if there was anything that could block my prayers from being answered. While going through a separation due to my husband's adultery, I knew there was a pretty good chance I needed to deal with one or more prayer blockers. I looked at these verses above and systematically examined each area. I needed to make sure my heart was clear of all bitterness, anger, and unforgiveness.

If we hold onto any of the pain, rejection, bitterness, or anger, these will block our line of communication to God. Our relationship will be broken. I can't imagine as a mother needing help for my children and not being able to ask for it.

To further understand a blocked line of communication to God, imagine this scene. My son gets into an accident. I see he needs help, as he is lying unresponsive with the possibility of dying. He desperately needs CPR, and since we are close to home, I whip out my phone to call our neighbor, the medic. I frantically search for his number, find it, and begin to dial. No response. I look down and realize there is no phone service—it dawns on me that ***I forgot to pay my phone bill.***

What a terrible situation! Here I am, the only person around that can get my son needed help, and there is nothing I can do. I cannot get him the help he needs simply because I neglected to pay my bill. I did not do what was necessary to keep the lines of communication open.

This scene is the same as what can happen with God and us. If we neglect to deal with any sin we commit or the negative emotions (that turn to sin) that come from the sins of others, we are failing to keep the lines of communication open. That, if nothing else, is a powerful reason to confess all my hurts associated with a painful separation or divorce. We all need to keep the lines of communication open between ourselves and our Creator, to maintain a close, intimate relationship with our Father who wants to help us in time of need.

Ways to Open Communication for Effective Prayers

While certain things, such as unforgiveness, disrespect to a spouse, and choosing not to reconcile with others, can block our communication to God, submitting our will to His can swing those doors wide open. We should always be willing to submit to God's will, placing it above our own. We see this prayer modeled by Jesus Christ in Luke 22:42, *"'Father, if thou be willing, remove this cup from me: nevertheless not my will, but thine, be done.'"* In Ephesians 6:6b, Paul encourages Christians to continue *"as the servants of Christ, doing the will of God from the heart."* Once our attitudes are in line with God's will and we've eliminated unforgiveness and sin, we can claim all the remarkable promises found in God's Word regarding prayer. But first, let's examine ways to know beyond a shadow of a doubt that our prayers are effective and being heard.

4 Steps to KNOW Our Prayers are Effective

- Submit to God's will
- Ask in Jesus' name
- Abide in God and in His Word
- Hold onto Faith without Doubt

Step #1: Submit to God's Will

When we submit to God's will, first and foremost, we are assured God will hear us. *"And this is the confidence that we have in him, that, if we ask any thing **according to his will**, he heareth us: And if we know that he hear us, whatsoever we ask, we know that we have the petitions that we desired of him"* (1 John 5:14-15). I think this is where so many of us slide off the path; at least I know I do. When something happens that we don't like, typically the first thing we do is ask God to fix it, change it, heal it, or remove it. One of the hardest things to do is pray for a situation to be handled according to "His will," not "our will," especially when we want to see a particular outcome, which is a normal reaction to a broken marriage, health concerns, or financial woes.

Our typical response is to immediately ask for what we want, what seems right to us. We enter into prayer expecting a positive outcome, we ask everyone to join us in prayer, and we truly pray, believing for a miracle. Often, we never once stop and *first* ask God what HIS will is for the situation or for the person. We just enter into prayer with our request and then get mad at God because He didn't answer our prayers.

I wonder what would happen to the disappointment rate when we run into the next major life event if we first ask God: "What is Your will?" and "How should I pray?" Then, knowing we are praying in His will, we ask others to join in waiting for God's plan to unfold, no matter if it is what we want or not. My hope is that I can say with conviction, *"Not my will but thine."*

Step #2: Ask in Jesus' Name

When we enter into prayer, we need to address the God who created us and has the power to help us. We must acknowledge Him and specifically ask Him for help. *"And whatsoever **ye shall ask in my name**, that will I do, that the Father may be glorified in the Son. If ye shall ask any thing in my name, I will do it"* (John 14:13-14).

Step #3: Abide in God and His Word

When we choose to listen to the Holy Spirit, walk in lockstep with Jesus Christ, and obey the Word of God, we can ask, and it will be done. *"'If ye **abide in me**, and **my words abide in you**, ye shall ask what ye will, and it shall be done unto you'"* (John 15:7).

I have to say this step can trip me up at times. I realized I can't be spewing out vile words against another person and still be "abiding" in Jesus. Even though that spouse or ex may deserve to receive "death by words," the grace of God will come out instead as we "abide (meno; to stay, remain, BE PRESENT) in Him" (Strong's). God is full of love, compassion, and mercy, and if I am present with Him, those things will flow out of me as well.

Step #4: Hold onto Faith without Doubt

The last step, and most likely one of the hardest to accomplish, is believing without doubting. *"Jesus answered and said unto them, 'Verily I say unto you, **If ye have faith, and doubt not**, ye shall not only do this which is done to the fig tree, but also if ye shall say unto this mountain, Be thou removed, and be thou cast into the sea; it shall be done'"* (Matthew 21:21). Our faith is our inheritance given to us through the power of the cross. When we doubt that faith, it takes away our power and renders us useless, so we cannot victoriously "move mountains." We must believe wholeheartedly!

PROMISE: *"'And all things, whatsoever ye shall ask in prayer, believing, ye shall receive.'" (*Matthew 21: 22)

Most of us are familiar with this promise. I don't know about you, but there have been times when I had a hard time believing it.

Throughout life, we will all encounter serious mountains which are obstacles that seem impossible to overcome. When we are in the midst of violent storms, when we feel like we're going downhill without any brakes, sometimes it feels like God is not listening and there is no way out. When we feel this way, when we see no way out, we must simply grab hold of our faith and believe that if we follow the steps below, they will be heard.

Below is a recap of what I have learned. Since I like to use sports analogies to lock a thought into my mind, I came up with the following Defensive/Offensive Steps to tackle God's instructions:

3 Defensive Steps to Unblock Prayers

- Ask God to forgive your sins and then forgive the sins of others
- Let go of disrespect and honor others
- Reconcile with anyone you have offended

4 Offensive Steps for Effective Prayers

- Submit to God's will and line your desires up with His
- Pray in Jesus Christ's name
- Abide in the truth of God's Word
- Have a faith that holds - without wavering

Then and only then will our prayers be heard. As I began to realize when God does or does not hear me, I set out to change my prayer life. I understood and accepted that the power of effective prayer is something I desperately want and need.

Just as I have the responsibility of putting on the whole armor of God, I also have the responsibility to learn proper methods for effective, powerful prayer.

The War Room: The Power of Effective Praying

One month before my husband walked out the door, we strolled into the movie theater on a date to watch *The War Room*. This movie tells of a couple, Tony and Elizabeth Jordan, who are struggling in their marriage. Elizabeth is a real estate agent who "just happens" to list the home of Miss Clara. Miss Clara is a spiritual giant, and she begins to mentor Elizabeth. Miss Clara takes Elizabeth to a closet in her home she has converted into her little oasis. It is a quiet and private sanctuary where she can go to get alone with God. She encourages Elizabeth to create her own sanctuary. Elizabeth takes her advice and creates her own quiet space in her walk-in-closet. She begins praying for her husband and child. At first, it doesn't seem like her prayers make any difference at all, yet she persists. Meanwhile, her husband, Tony, is off flirting with other women.

As the movie unfolds, you see Elizabeth's prayers do, in fact, affect her husband's life. Elizabeth knows he is playing the field, yet she never confronts him. Instead, she goes to her "war room,"

Power Of Effective Prayer

her prayer closet, and pours out her heart to an all-knowing God who knows best how to handle this situation. On the night Tony is going to take that final step and commit adultery, he "unexpectedly" gets food poisoning, causing him to return home without participating in any hanky-panky. Being stopped before he could "seal the deal" gives him time to think about his actions. He becomes reflective and does not call that woman again. Now that is a turn of events!

Elizabeth's prayers were quite effective, don't you think? I know, I know, that devilish little imp on your shoulder is snickering and saying, "Ha...serves you right, man! You ought to know better than to mess around on your wife! If all you got was a little food poisoning, you got off easy." But seriously, if that had been you or me, what would we have done? What do you think would have happened if we had confronted our spouse in that situation? Would our words have had the same effect? I know for certain that I could not have achieved a better outcome than that from the conviction by the Holy Spirit. So why, for crying out loud, if we know the perfect Holy Spirit can handle any situation flawlessly, do we constantly insert our imperfect selves hoping for a better outcome? Sometimes throughout this whole process, I felt like I was starring Me, Myself, and I in a movie called *Dumb, Dumber and Dumbest*! It's hard to let go and let God, that's for sure!

Back to the story plot. Tony does not commit adultery, but it is not a fairy tale ending. His personal life hits an all-time low followed directly by a decline in his business life, due to his inappropriate actions. Instead of beating him down further, his wife extends grace and forgiveness. When he gets a dose of true unconditional love, it breaks down his pride, and he seeks her forgiveness. Together, the two of them pray and support each other as he works to repair the damage and make the situation right. He apologizes to his boss and rectifies the situation to the best of his ability. Then they pray and wait for God to work. Life does not miraculously get better instantly, but they now have the strength of God holding them. Now they are a three-fold cord, standing strong together, just the way God intends.

Here was my problem: as inspiring as this movie was, I never took the time to create a war room (a prayer room) of my own. Sometimes, I wonder what might have happened if I had heeded the warning God gave me through that movie and taken prayer more seriously. While I didn't bother to create a special prayer place at that time, rest assured I have one now. I highly recommend the movie, and I highly recommend having a war room of your own.

A war room or prayer closet is really just a place in your home where you can go to be alone with God, where you can pour out your heart and listen to His. Conversations with God are where we find true power, not the actual room itself. It is there the Great Judge renders His verdicts and there where changes occur. Battles are waged on our knees, during our alone time with God! Whether you use a special room, a closet, your back porch, your kids' treehouse, or just a corner of your kitchen, great things can happen there. It must only be quiet, away from distractions, so you can fully and openly communicate with God. Personally, I use a closet; when I'm in there, no one can see the sniffling, sobbing mess I make while I cry out to Jesus! My red eyes and swollen face, covered with snot and tears, just wouldn't be good for my image. For those reasons alone, I love my actual prayer closet, which, for me, is and always will remain behind closed doors!

Our Example

Everything Jesus did in the New Testament during His ministry happened through prayer. If He is our example, which He should be, then let's follow Jesus' example and pray as He did. Attempting to pray as Jesus did, I gave myself a little challenge. I made a commitment that before I told anyone else my problem, I was going to pray about it first. I was going to write it on my prayer board and ask for wisdom. More often than not, I did not feel prompted to DO anything. Amazingly enough, God would work out the situation. I was able to appreciate and applaud the outcome as one would a famous Broadway play. That was a life-changing challenge. Once I began to change my thinking and go to my war room to win my battles, peace and healing came over me in waves.

The Lord accomplishes so many wonderful things through prayer, affecting change and stirring up answers long with blessings. Here are a handful of examples of what effective prayer can do:

Shattered Souls Made Whole

- Prayer can defeat the devil (Luke 22:32)
- Prayer is the way for lost souls to be found (Luke 18:13)
- Prayer allows us to acquire wisdom (James 1:5)
- Prayer is the way to restoration (James 5:16-20)
- Prayer is the way to be strengthened (Jude 1:20, Matthew 26:41)
- Prayer sends missionaries out (Matthew 9:38)
- Prayer offers provision for our needs (Matthew 6:11)
- Prayer is the way for our sins to be forgiven (Matthew 6:12)
- Prayer leads us away from temptation (Matthew 6:11-13)
- Prayer heals the sick (James 5:16)

I have to stop and wonder what our world would look like if every professing Christian really understood what can happen if we continually wield the weapon of effective prayer. Maybe those of us reading this can start a powerful prayer movement: #EffectivePrayer #PrayerPower.

Praise, Prayer, and Bible Reading

Once I started using my prayer closet every day, I realized another amazing component to powerful, effective prayer. We are to enter God's presence with praise and thanksgiving first, before asking for anything: "Enter into His gates with thanksgiving, *and* into His courts with praise: be thankful unto Him, *and* bless His name" (Psalm 100:4). It is easy to give praise to God after He answers or

Power Of Effective Prayer

gives us a blessing, but how many of us praise Him before that, in faithful anticipation of His goodness and promises? Often, I fail to thank Him for answering prayers before I see the results. Recently I ran across one of my favorite, yet uncommon, Bible stories. It's the story of King Jehoshaphat where he did, in fact, give praise before the victory.

> *Tomorrow go ye down against them... Ye shall not need to fight in this battle: set yourselves, stand ye still, and see the salvation of the Lord with you, O Judah and Jerusalem: fear not, nor be dismayed; tomorrow go out against them: for the Lord will be with you. And Jehoshaphat bowed his head with his face to the ground: and all Judah and the inhabitants of Jerusalem fell before the Lord, worshipping the Lord...and as they went forth, Jehoshaphat stood and said, Hear me, O Judah, and ye inhabitants of Jerusalem; Believe in the Lord your God, so shall ye be established; believe His prophets, so shall ye prosper. And when he had consulted with the people, he appointed singers unto the Lord, and that should praise the beauty of holiness, as **they went out before the army**, and to say, Praise the Lord; for His mercy endureth forever. **And when they began to sing and to praise, the Lord set ambushments against the children** of Ammon, Moab, and Mount Seir, which were come against Judah; and they were smitten (2 Chronicles 20:16-22).*

I can't help but chuckle as I imagine the faces of the enemy when they realized they had been beaten by singers! Of course, it doesn't specifically say the singers set the ambush, but their melodies did cause that ambush to occur. I'm curious to find out what would happen if we would sing. Would our praise be strong enough to cause the enemy to falter and fail? The enemy could be using a family member, a crotchety mother-in-law, your neighbor, or your spouse, to get under your skin and try every last nerve you have. When you have one of those out-of-body moments that come from your last nerve being hit, do something for me – SING! Read, out loud, your favorite Psalm declaring who God is. Send up some love to your heavenly Daddy. Then send me an email and tell me how it turns out!

See, when I comprehended the power that comes with approaching the throne of God correctly, with thanksgiving and praise, I now start my time with God by singing or speaking my praise. Sometimes I log onto YouTube to listen and sing along to my mix of favorite praise and worship videos. I thank God for who He is. Then I begin singing to Him which prepares my heart to honestly hear from Him. As I praise God for who He is, sometimes the praise comes in the form of a song, a Psalm, or whatever is in my own heart and mind at that particular time.

After praising Him, I take my time confessing any known sins. Then I ask God to *"Search me, O God, and know my heart: try me, and know my thoughts: And see if there be any wicked way in me"*

(Psalm 139:23-24). I want to make sure that any issues I have not dealt with come to light so I can handle them appropriately. The trick is to wait quietly and long enough so the Holy Spirit's *"still small voice"* can come through the crowded clutter of my mind. That war room is filled with all my talks with God—as if He is sitting right in front of me as my best friend. Finally, as I open His Word, my mind is clear and my heart is ready to receive. Remember when we pray, we are speaking to God. When we read the Bible that is God speaking to us.

When we make an effort to place a time of praising God at the beginning of our quiet time, then enter into prayer and follow that up with Bible reading, these acts will bring about healing and an amazing peace. I have learned to allow the Holy Spirit to direct my quiet time with Him. My devotional time has come alive, causing my prayers to be answered, my broken heart to be mended, and a peace to flood my soul...all because I've learned the best process for communicating with God.

An Effective Tactic

Have you ever struggled during your prayer time and found that your mind wandered off? I have both hands raised right now because that often happened to me. I am excited to share that I found an effective prayer tactic. Here it goes, and you have to promise not to laugh... I pray out loud. Yep, it's true! This tactic helps me tremendously, and I've found a funny thing happens when

I pray out loud... my mind does not wander. Perhaps you've been frustrated when your brain takes a field trip while praying! Maybe you start thinking of your never-ending to-do list, or all the worries and situations you have to deal with. Before you know it, ten minutes go by, and you realize you haven't really said a word to God but have only had a conversation with yourself. Praying out loud is an effective method to help you concentrate. A word of caution: just remember to ALWAYS DO THIS BEHIND CLOSED DOORS. When you pray out loud behind closed doors, it lowers the chances of you getting carted off in a straitjacket behind another set of closed doors known as the crazy house!

Seriously though, praising God, praying out loud, and Bible reading change things. Now that we have a better understanding of what brings about effective prayer, we may just need to make a few modifications. If you are like me, realizing these changes needed to be made caused me to think, "Bummer, all this time and I have not been effective. Well, shoot!" I have good news for you. It maybe we were not *always* off base—just sometimes. It's like sending a rocket to the moon. Apparently, more often than not that rocket was off course. It did not stay on an exact line as intended. Over and over again, it slides off to the left or right, and NASA had to make adjustments to the trajectory to bring it back onto the correctly plotted course. That is the same with us and prayer. There are times when we slide off-course, get sidetracked, distracted, or stop listening. Don't get discouraged thinking all your past prayers were useless. We all tend to slide off course at times. But like the rocket headed to the moon, it eventually got there and so will we!

When we slide off course, if we submit to God's will, He will reset our trajectory by preparing a special message specifically for each one of us. That message, whether through Scripture, a pastor's preaching, praise and prayer time, or a song, will bring us back on the proper course. Being "on course" in our Christian lives means living with the destination of a holy filled, intimate life with God. I crave that intimacy with Him. That can only come through effective, quiet, and reflective time alone with God.

Available: One-on-One Expert Life-Changing Consultations

I was recently at a conference for authors and speakers. Over the years, as a real estate agent, small business owner, a ministry layperson, and now as an author, I have attended numerous seminars and workshops to grow my knowledge in a variety of areas. This particular seminar was teaching a bit of everything from great writing ideas to marketing and publishing.

In the audience, there were new authors, alongside authors who had one or several books published. Those authors had achieved a certain level of success. I noticed new authors, who had not published anything yet, would seek out those who had forged the way and understood more about the process than they did. They tried to soak up any and all information about how to make it or how to overcome certain hurdles. Then, of course, the speakers themselves were the ones that had "made it" in some way or another, and everyone was vying for their attention.

One evening there were several radio hosts, publishers, and book coaches who were invited to be there. We were given a two-and-a-half-minute opportunity to "pitch" them our idea. If we presented well and they liked our book or speaking topics, they would give us their business card with instructions on how to proceed to the next step. That was a fantastic opportunity, but we all wanted more. We wanted more help, more guidance, and a personalized plan for us.

Imagine you are sitting at that seminar, just soaking it all up. This thought enters your mind, "Man, if I could just have a few moments of time with that expert, I would be able to know what to do, which direction to go, what pitfalls to avoid. I would love to get a *foolproof customized* plan for me from someone who is a higher authority."

The third day of the seminar, the host speaker made us a business offer: "For those who would like to sign up, we are offering a one-on-one consultation for a WHOLE DAY with this expert." *Wow, what an opportunity!* I thought to myself. *Maybe the high cost doesn't matter because everything I learn is going to catapult me forward towards my dream more quickly and easily. Days, weeks, and months of trial and error can be avoided if I will JUST listen to this expert,* the voice in my head whispered.

As I was thinking about how wonderful it would be to get that one-on-one opportunity, we were dismissed for a break. I decided to go to my room to read my Bible and pray since I had missed it that morning. I got right into praying and conversing with the Highest Authority I know. I began with praising my heavenly Father.

"Lord, You are my Savior, Redeemer, the Righteous Judge, and Creator of heaven and earth. I love You, God."

I was on a roll. My thoughts just kept flowing out of me, and I continued to speak out loud praising God.

"Lord, You know everything before it even happens. You created something out of nothing. You have more creative genius in the tip of Your fingernail than anyone could ever begin to imagine."

That is when it hit me – here I was thinking about how awesome it would be to get a WHOLE DAY in the presence of an expert. One who would help guide and direct me, but in reality, I had that ability already. I could walk into the presence of God anytime I wanted through prayer. HE is the expert, the creative genius, the Creator of this world we see and can't see. I GET to have a one-on-one with Him anytime I want. Who better to guide and direct me but the Heavenly Father who loves me, knows my destiny, and knows the plans He has for me, the One who can see into the future? Of course, we still need others to teach us in our fields; I am not discounting them at all. Yet, I stand in awe of God and who He is. Amazing! Right in reach is the Almighty God who has ALL the answers I need to guide me down the right path. I just have to sign up! I have to decide I want His expert guidance and then plan a time to be totally absorbed in Him, expecting direction as He pours out His wisdom and guidance to me as promised in James 1:5.

I could just imagine an announcement to an event where God was the keynote speaker, and He was offering a one-on-one consultation. Maybe it would read something like this:

Sign up for A One-On-One Consultation - 8 hours with Jehovah God:

The Reigning King of Kings, the Top Scientist, Expert Parent, the Great Physician, Great Adventurer and Explorer, Number One Artist and Sculptor, Author of the Number One Best-Selling Book, The Bible, Foremost Expert on Theology and Sci-Fi (see the Book of Revelation), Most Righteous Judge ....

Oh, my word! Every single day, I GET to stand before this Greatest of Speakers, Presenters, and Publishers. I get to "pitch" to Him. I get to listen to all His wisdom and knowledge for my particular dreams and destiny. I get to soak up ANY greatness that He has to share with me on which way to go if I only choose to ask. What if I did that every day? Would I follow through on the action items He gave me? Would I then be called the greatest protégé' of Jesus Christ who ever walked the earth?

What about you? What field of work are you in? Are you a professional homemaker, business owner, or sales representative? Your job requires a particular set of expertise. If you could meet a famous person in your line of work right now, who would that be? What would you hope to gain?

What if we changed our thinking? What if we started thinking about God our Father, Jesus Christ our Savior, and the Holy Spirit as our Guide and *first* seek out a one-on-one Consultation every day with Him? Would your world change? Would you gain wisdom? Prayer does change things, but you and I have to be willing to pray the way Jesus Christ prayed and follow His expert counsel received from His Word.

As we struggle through this painful experience of separation or divorce, I can think of no greater One to help me through than the Heart Doctor, the Great Physician, Jesus Christ who has armed us with effective ways to pray for positive change. I found that because of my prayer time, I was strengthened and encouraged. God gave me the ideas and guidance I needed to get through that day and the next. I was in a vulnerable position. My mind was not thinking straight. I once was so very broken, yet God healed my heart that had shattered into a million pieces. Prayer time gave me the resolve to continue living for God, putting one step in front of the other, as I adjusted my course daily. In doing so, God gave me a peace, a hope, and a calmness that came only from Him. And for the brokenhearted, it can help each of us to let go and let God heal all our sorrows.

My Journal:

---·❋·---

"There are so many changes happening in my life. I don't know what to do about all of them, and it's somewhat overwhelming. I still don't understand why God seems silent at times, but I have just to be still and know that He is God. I will praise Him through the storms, whether I feel like it or not. God, You are so good to me, providing for the kids and me every day. I praise You for Your continued hedge of protection around my family and me spiritually, physically, and emotionally. You are a good, good Father."

---·❋·---

HEALING TOOLS

Memorize Scripture: *"If ye abide in me, and my words abide in you, ye shall ask what ye will, and it shall be done unto you"* (John 15:7).

Meditate on the Journal of Psalms: *"I will praise thee, O Lord, with my whole heart; I will shew forth all thy marvelous works. I will be glad and rejoice in thee: I will sing praise to thy name, O thou most High"* (Psalm 9:1-2).

Praise Daily and Often: Lord, thank You for giving me the Scriptures, filled with all the keys I need to help me understand how to pray effectively.

Prayer Decree: Help me to dedicate time every day to really talk with You, as well as listen. I praise You for Your blessings and guidance, even if I cannot see the results yet.

Focused Thought: Prayer is the moving force for positive change

Lesson 6

Handling Regret and Overcoming Depression

"O Lord, rebuke me not in thine anger, neither chasten me in thy hot displeasure. Have mercy upon me, O Lord; for I am weak: O Lord, heal me; for my bones are vexed. My soul is also sore vexed: but thou, O Lord, how long? Return, O Lord, deliver my soul: oh save me for thy mercies' sake" (Psalm 6:1-4).

Words echo through my mind as I reflect on my past mistakes and experiences of the last three years.

If I only had known then what I know now.

If only I had not chased my husband trying to figure out what was wrong.

Handling Regret And Overcoming Depression

If only I had not sent those emails.

If only I had not given him 25% of my income in the following 5 weeks after he left.

If only I had listened to my friends and counselors.

If only I had not done THAT embarrassing thing.

If only…

REGRET. A 6-letter word that feels more like a four-letter swear word

Let's talk about regret.

So often regret causes us to hang our head in shame. Regret can trigger a nosedive onto the bed with our head buried deep under the covers and a burning desire never to get up. Maybe I am the only one with regrets, but I have a sneaky suspicion anyone who has gone through a separation or divorce has also pulled a few crazy stunts. Maybe your regrets are not as well-known as the Janet Jackson Super Bowl wardrobe malfunction, Tiger Woods' infidelities, or Jimmy Swaggart's infamous confession, but they are still yours and they weigh on you.

Maybe the whole world did not see your specific meltdowns or mistakes, but those regrets are documented in your world and certainly in your own mind. That movie reel in our heads keeps playing that fateful moment over and over, and it never changes, it never gets better. That is the moment when you wish, as a friend of mine suggested, we could take the memory stick from the movie, *Men in Black*, and make it all go away. Just look at the flash of light coming from the magical device and WAH LAA…your memory and that other person's memory are wiped clean. In its place is the newly concocted story. Boy, wouldn't that be sweet? Someone please, please, create that device now!

Of course, that's not going to happen. But we can take steps which will lead us to make better decisions in the heat of the moment. That way we'll avoid having to deal with regretful actions in the first place.

If you read the verses from Psalm 6 at the beginning of this chapter, you can probably relate to feeling "vexed," meaning troubled, provoked.

I was curious to see if my regrets that troubled me were unique to just myself or if they also applied to others, so I decided to research "regrets after breakups." After reading different posts, thinking of my own, along with watching friends or others engage in one or more regretful actions, I compiled a list. These exploits seem to be consistently at the top of the list and are the "go to" choices, whether the person was a man or a woman:

- Posting a slam against your spouse or ex on a social media site
- Changing something drastic on your body
- Trying too hard to get your spouse back
- Stalking your spouse or ex
- Faking a pregnancy to win him back
- Getting wasted and/or having a quick one-night stand with some random stranger or a friend
- Engaging in alcohol, drugs, prescription medicine, or over-the-counter medicines

Do any of these actions sound familiar? You are not alone in your mistakes or regrets. We all do crazy things or have what I call "out of character" moments. David of the Old Testament had several "crazy" moments. Still, he was remembered as a "man after God's own heart." If David could make so many mistakes and be filled with regrets like the ones we read about in the book of Psalm, yet still be known as close to God, then there is hope for us!

Let's look at an unforgettable blunder David made: Here is a story of David when he acted a little, okay, A LOT, off his rocker:

"And David...was sore afraid of Achish the king of Gath. And he changed his behaviour before them, and feigned himself mad in their hands, and scrabbled on the doors of the gate, and let his spittle fall down upon his beard. Then said Achish unto his servants,

Lo, ye see the man is mad: wherefore then have ye brought him to me? Have I need of mad men, that ye have brought this fellow to play the mad man in my presence? Shall this fellow come into my house? David therefore departed thence, and escaped to the cave Adullam" (1 Samuel 21:12-22:1).

See? He seriously needed a mental health day! He began acting so mad he actually let drool and spit come out of his mouth, landing on his beard as he clawed at the doors. Could you imagine letting go like that? Well, in David's defense he thought it was what he needed to do in order to save his life. That is what I call some serious "thinking on his feet," or was it? Sometimes, we see only one solution to a problem and we "think on our feet" without seeking advice from others or at the very least sleeping on it.

When I look further in Scripture, I see it is filled with very human people who reacted in the moment, overtaken by feelings, and then regretted their actions. I think of Moses who killed someone; David sleeping with Bathsheba then ordering the death of her husband; Peter's denial of Christ; and Paul's persecution of Christians before his conversion.

There are many more people in Scripture we could name. Maybe you can think of some as you are reading. But the main thing to notice is that every single one of these people went on to be used by God in powerful ways. We remember their faith, not their failures.

Handling Regret And Overcoming Depression

In an earlier lesson we looked at how Peter, after his denial of Christ, was reinstated by Christ to be used in the church going forward. In the same way, we too can be restored after our regretful behavior. He can redeem us, just like He did Peter. We can move forward knowing God will use us.

Paul, knowing firsthand the pain that comes with regrettable actions, says this about moving forward, *"Brethren, I count not myself to have apprehended: but this one thing I do, forgetting those things which are behind, and reaching forth unto those things which are before, I press toward the mark for the prize of the high calling of God in Christ Jesus"* (Philippians 3:13-14).

> We may have too many regrets to mention, yet we have a God who redeems us.

We may have too many regrets to mention, yet we have a God who redeems us. *"In whom we have redemption through his blood, the forgiveness of sins, according to the riches of his grace"* (Ephesians 1:7). God loves and cares for us just as we love and care for our children even when they don't do the right thing. God wants us to rely on Him to get through the hard parts so He can fill us with peace.

Our hearts have been trampled on, bruised, and broken. In the process, we can react like wounded and cornered animals, snapping at anyone who crosses our path. We know we are overreacting, yet at the time we can't seem to stop saying or doing things we later regret. Let's turn to God, knowing He will "keep" our hearts. *"The peace of God, which passeth all understanding, shall keep your hearts and minds through Christ Jesus"* (Philippines 4:7).

Below are five guidelines that may help prevent knee-jerk reactions. I wish I had these posted in my house to read daily the first year of my separation.

5 Guidelines for Avoiding Regretful Actions

Because of my many regretful lapses, I developed some guiding principles when I knew I was overly emotional, whether it was feeling hurt or mad. We can use these guidelines to avoid ever reacting in ways that will lead to regret.

Instead of reacting, we can condition ourselves to be proactive and avoid those situations. Being proactive means being aware of our triggers then avoiding them. We'll discuss triggers in more depth in the next lesson. For now, understand triggers are those things that make you react in regretful ways.

Guideline #1: Avoid Reacting: Sleep Before Taking Action

If I had had the "I must sleep before acting" rule in place at the beginning of the separation, I would have handled things so very differently and possibly had fewer regrets. When going through a break up, our emotions are heightened. When we become anxious or must deal with stressful events, it can cause our bodies to pump adrenaline. In turn, this causes us to feel nervous or jittery and our hearts begin to race. It is hard to think clearly with adrenaline running through our bloodstream. Waiting until we are in a calm state will help us to think rationally.

Guideline #2: Avoid Sending Texts or Emails at the End of the Day

Here is a free piece of advice learned firsthand by yours truly: NEVER, EVER send an email after 8 p.m. during a traumatic event! All of my emotional moments came in the evening when the weight of life's upheavals seemed overwhelming. It would always start out with me journaling my feelings and somewhere along the way, that little "drunk money" (who appeared so many times without even a hint of alcohol) perched on my shoulder would say, "OOOOOH… that is good…you should email that well-stated piece of literary work to so and so." NOT a good idea!

At the end of the day, after dealing with stressors and responsibilities, we can be tired, worn down, and vulnerable. Those written messages sent via texts, emails, or other avenues like this, cannot be taken back. Once they're out there, they're out there. They're final. Sending an overly emotional text or email can just compound the regrets we already have.

Guideline #3: Avoid Social Media

A friend of mine who has gone through a divorce cannot look at social media because it triggers sadness. When she looks, all she sees is seemingly happy couples and families, and it seems to magnify her aloneness. Maybe being on social media will tempt you to look up your ex, or someone your ex is involved with. That's probably not going to lead down a good path.

Ask yourself, what is the purpose of going on these social media sites? Then ask yourself why you need to do that, three or four times, until you get to the real reason you feel the need to check on that person. What good can come of it?

Guideline #4: Avoid Acting Before Phoning a Friend

Being "in my head" for too long was never a good thing. In the beginning of my separation, I had to deal with a multitude of hard topics. At times, I attempted to process a problem by myself. When I became introverted, I found it was just not productive. I am an audible processor and the best way for me to figure out the problem, then a solution, is to verbalize it.

I had a few friends who were there when I called. Often, they talked me down off a ledge. When I got angry, was extremely hurt, or had to deal with high levels of stress, irrational thinking got the best of me. I learned to activate the "Phone a Friend" card. Showing enough sense to throw out that card, call a friend, vent out my frustrations, and then ask them for advice were invaluable steps.

You may also need to process audibly so you can get to the proper conclusion or maybe you are the one who figures it all out in your head. I can say with assurance that either method is okay, but enacting that final decision will be best after running it by a wise friend or counselor. Let them help you sort out what is logical, what is a good idea, and what is just plain crazy.

Guideline #5: Avoid Alcohol or Mood-Altering Substances

I am not an expert on the subject of alcohol, but I know many people who have stories about their regrets from acting while uninhibited. They regret drinking and acting in a way they normally would not. On alcohol.org we find, "Alcohol can…lower your inhibitions and increase impulsivity, making it hard for you to consider potential consequences of your actions."

Research shows that alcohol decreases some of the activity of the prefrontal cortex. This part of the brain is what helps us to think clearly and rationally, and it's involved in our decision-making abilities. Alcohol disrupts these processes, often leading us to act without thinking.

Even knowing the downfalls of what alcohol could do, I still wanted desperately to binge so I could forget for just one night. The thought crossed my mind many times. Knowing the facts above and since alcoholism runs in my family, I was scared I would become dependent on alcohol to cope, so I chose to never touch it. Whenever it crossed my mind to get a drink, I would pray that God would give me the strength to get through.

As you read later in this chapter, you will see that I did choose to use over-the-counter drugs. The results of either drugs, over-the-counter or otherwise, and alcohol are the same. They provide a temporary fix, and there is no guarantee you won't get addicted or hurt further. I implore you to pray for wisdom, and then seek help from a counselor or friend before succumbing to mood-altering substances.

It is okay to admit you want to use them; it's okay to be human. One of the enemy's tricks is to convince us to keep our desires hidden. As if hiding them will make them go away! It will not. *"For there is nothing covered, that shall not be revealed; neither hid, that shall not be known"* (Luke 12:2).

Once we admit we want a certain thing, if we take that desire to God, examine whether it is right or wrong, if it is of God or our flesh, then we can deal with it. We can ask for God to renew our minds and help us adjust our thinking. *"Search me, O God, and know my heart: try me, and know my thoughts,"* (Psalm 139:23). We must take control of our thoughts.

Unchecked Regret Leads to Depression

Regret...it sneaks into our minds...it taunts, it jeers... it is perched right on our shoulder where we can't help but hear the accusations loud and clear. Regret, shame, guilt...those are words that become "little drunk monkeys" that believe they have the right to speak into our lives. However, letting these thoughts linger can lead us to an even worse place.

Handling Regret And Overcoming Depression

Regret left unchecked can create wounds on the soul. For some the wounds will manifest as bitterness, vengefulness, or hopelessness. But many will experience one of the most common results of unchecked regret…depression.

This was the case for me, as my wounds manifested themselves as a cycle of depression. When I was depressed, my mind was busy chronicling the laundry list of my mistakes or the mistakes of others who deeply hurt me. A "woe-is-me" mental attitude began to spring up within me. So, my regrets fed the depression and the depression fed into more memories of more regrets. I realized that memories of personal regrets, guilt and, shame can trigger depression and maybe even suicidal thoughts.

Let's get into the area of our minds where the raw, ugly, painful thoughts are kept. Thoughts we desperately want to keep hidden from the world. For just a moment, let's go to that door—you know the one. That door you open only in the dead of night when no one is around, when you're absolutely certain no one can hear the screaming thoughts as the door cracks open.

Let's discuss thoughts of depression and suicide.

First, let me say this, If you are having suicidal thoughts, you need to tell someone. You need to seek help from a counselor or doctor or friend. Don't just say to yourself that the suicidal thoughts will go away. They might, but they might not. SEEK HELP!

I'm going to be very honest. I struggled for many months with depression and suicidal thoughts. Depression starts with just a thought. It begins with thoughts of regret, hurt, rejection, or some other thought and snowballs. Unchecked, these thoughts spiral out of control.

When my husband left, I fell into a deep depression. I was unable to eat or sleep, and I was barely functioning mentally. I'm going to open one of my doors. I want you to know you are not alone and there is hope.

Journal Entry: November 25, 2015

"Thanksgiving Eve, I took a sleeping pill. The next morning, I got up at eight a.m., took some Benadryl and slept until two p.m. I got up for a few hours, and around nine p.m., I took another sleeping pill. I found myself counting the hours until I could go to bed, just so I could end the nightmare. I looked for ways to pack my days with stuff, just to forget and focus on something else. I am so deeply hurt. I don't understand how a Christian can just walk away without any warning, without even trying—no counseling or anything—just gone. I thought to myself, "I have had it! I need to finish my will. I have had enough of the constant pain, sleeplessness, and memories replaying over and over in my mind."

The very next day my friend used her house key and let herself in. She walked right in my room and said, "Get up! Figure out a way to live without your husband and move on. I've never seen you this way. Your husband's not coming back, but you're a strong woman. You have so much to give, and your children need you, so get yourself together and figure out a way to make it through."

My friend's intervention helped me at that moment, yet waves of depression kept sweeping over me throughout the next few months. I remember times when I would be walking along thinking about my next task, and BOOM…the bottom would drop out of my stomach. It was as if I was on a roller coaster, and I had just taken a 200-foot drop—my stomach lurched. I would also be jerked out of sleep with that same feeling. It was terrible. I didn't know how to stop it, and it led to severe depression which led to suicidal thoughts. I just couldn't take the pain, the uncertainty, anymore.

One of the first times I had a thought of ending it all occurred when I was driving down the road. I was thinking about my life and the pain I was feeling. I felt I could not go on one more day.

Like a flash, a fleeting thought blew through my mind: *If I truly want to stop the pain, all I have to do is pull the wheel and drive into the guardrail.* I could end the pain with a jerk of the wheel.

A few days later, I was jogging down the road, and as I ran across a bridge, I stopped. I looked down at the oncoming highway traffic and thought, *Boy, all I have to do is jump… it will be all over, in a blink of an eye, with just one jump.*

Another time I asked my estranged husband for my gun. I wanted to keep all my "options" open. Finally, I realized I needed help.

I did what I needed to do and went to the doctor. I was given a prescription for a mild antidepressant. In my heart I didn't want to take the medicine, but I didn't know what else to do. I filled the prescription, and although I didn't feel any relief immediately, I had been assured by my doctor that in about two weeks I would feel a difference. My doctor explained that medicine was not a quick fix and not a cure-all. She encouraged me to seek counseling as well. I called a Christian counselor and scheduled an appointment.

Before we move on, let me say a word or two about antidepressants. Christians can have mixed feelings about taking them. I understand that. Each of you, with the guidance of wise counsel, prayer, and advice from your doctor, must decide what to do concerning taking medicine or supplements. I personally only stayed on them for a little over a month as I was praying, seeking counseling and getting a handle on the power of my mind. I found situational depression could be controlled by changing the negative patterns of my thoughts. No matter what you decide, I believe ultimately, we will find lasting healing by processing our wounds with the Lord.

In the meantime, I desperately wanted the thoughts to go away. I hadn't learned yet what would make them go away for good. That was several months away.

All these damaging thoughts rolled through my head, almost constantly.

One thing I knew, I could not be alone with my own thoughts! I felt I was always playing a defensive position. I felt I never got ahead.

Handling Regret And Overcoming Depression

I had formed a very bad habit of letting those thoughts sit there marinating. Now I had to replace those damaging habits with beneficial ones. I needed to go on the offense.

Techniques to Combat Depression and Suicidal Thoughts

Regret and depression have a common denominator: they each begin in our minds. We need to deal with regret and depression, just like we do all the other soul wounds.

I think the hardest part of regret and depression is forgiving ourselves, letting go, and giving all those regrets and depressing thoughts to Jesus Christ. We have the power through the Holy Spirit to take control back over our minds. One specific Scripture gives us a strategy for these harmful thoughts. That Scripture is 2 Corinthians 10:5, *"Casting down imaginations, and every high thing that exalteth itself against the knowledge of God, **and bringing into captivity every thought to the obedience of Christ.**"*

> We have the power through the Holy Spirit to take control back over our minds.

This Scripture tells us we are to take our thoughts captive to the obedience of Christ. So what does that mean in real life? How do we take our thoughts captive? I found the following practical applications for taking my thoughts captive. Each of these can make a difference in our healing and our ability to move past negative thoughts.

- Identify the lies from Satan
- Fill our minds with the truth of Scripture
- Declare Jesus' name
- Fill our minds with godly music
- Read/Watch others' stories of triumph
- Find ways to laugh
- Find community
- Care for ourselves physically

Quickly Identify Satan's lies

Besides all the regrets clawing at my mind, there was one lie constantly whispered in my ear. It said, "You are not enough." The modified version said, "You are not good enough." Over and over that despair of not being good enough kept coming up. I felt like a piece of garbage tossed aside. Not only had one man rejected me but, now a second man. I was nothing. I was worthless.

In an earlier chapter we discussed spiritual warfare. It is real and it is harmful. Remember Satan is a liar, as we are told in John 8:44, *"...for he is a liar, and the father of it."*

All sorts of lies might roam through your head. Here are a few more I experienced:

If I had been a better wife, this wouldn't have happened.
Because I wasn't enough, my kids will suffer and be damaged.

I need to pack up and move away where no one will know who I am.
My kids and family will be better off without me.
I am going to be financially ruined.

Becoming aware that some of our thoughts could be lies coming at us from Satan is the first step in counteracting the spiral into negative thoughts.

"Keep (guard) thy heart with all diligence; for out of it are the issue of life" (Proverbs 4:23).

Fill our minds with the truth of Scripture

My own negative thoughts were one of the main reasons I spiraled down. Instead of letting our thoughts spiral, we take them captive by replacing them with the truth of Scripture. We can read Scripture, listen to Scripture being read aloud, or turn on some preaching.

When we have a negative thought, we line it up with God's Words. If it doesn't line up, then it's not from God. Find Scriptures to combat the lies. For example, when you are feeling fearful, fill your mind with the truth of 2 Timothy 1:7. *"For God hath not given us the spirit of fear; but of power, and of love, and of sound mind."*

I often turned on some preaching. I had recently heard a dynamic sermon regarding Peter. God later used that message to penetrate my wounded mind at just the right time. Friends would also send me links to preachers. Since I had Christian friends from all walks and backgrounds, an interesting dynamic occurred. I listened to a variety of men from slightly varied viewpoints. I listened to men such as Charles Stanley, Dr. David Jeremiah, Kenneth Copeland, and Steven Furtick. I may not agree with every doctrinal point of all these preachers, but I am a firm believer that you don't throw the baby out with the bathwater. God used their words to penetrate my heart. I was hearing Scripture I'd heard my whole life taught with a fresh perspective. I was always taught the Word of God is living and breathing. Through this experience I saw that God's Word did indeed come alive in ways I was easily able to apply to my life.

Declare Jesus' name

When I could not turn on the radio or grab my Bible, I would literally just speak out loud the name of Jesus. I suppose if you had been a fly on the wall in my house, you would have thought I had a touch of the crazy in me (a little like David), as I whispered the name of Jesus over and over again, but it worked. I am weak on my own, but if I follow in the footsteps of Jesus, I will have power to overcome, just as He did. 2 Corinthians 13:4 tells us, *"For though he was crucified through weakness, yet he liveth by the power of God. For we also are weak in him, but we shall live with him by the power of God toward you."* This same truth is found in Romans

10:13. *"For whosoever shall call upon the name of the Lord shall be saved."*

Fill our spirits with music

Each time I would feel the bottom drop out of my stomach or a harmful thought cross my mind, I found another effective technique was to turn on the Christian radio station or YouTube.

I listened to certain songs that helped me continually call on the name of Jesus. Those songs enabled me to remember the power He had and then gives us because He died on the cross and rose again. He did that in order to release that same power to me through the Holy Spirit.

One song, in particular, is entitled "Break Every Chain" by Will Reagan. It reminds us there is power in the name of Jesus and because of that powerful name the chains of depression and regret will be released. Freedom can be obtained, in our minds, if we call on the name of Jesus.

I asked God to wash away the evil thoughts that were coming into my mind. I listened to songs that spoke about the blood of Jesus, for I wanted reminders of the power of the blood. I really like Selah's song, "O the Blood." Singing these words washed the negative thoughts from my mind, as I claimed the power of the blood over my life. It is in the blood of Jesus we receive victory.

Shattered Souls Made Whole

Read/watch others' stories of triumph

The power of others' victorious stories to help us take thoughts captive can truly jettison us past being stuck in negativity.

I recently watched the documentary, *Natascha Kampusch: The Whole Story*, which shows how two people refused to let their circumstances overtake them. Instead, they controlled their minds and didn't allow the negativity of others to overshadow their positive thoughts.

This is a story of Australian Natascha Maria Kampusch. At the age of ten years old, on March 2, 1998, her mother watched her walk towards school, not knowing that day would change the course of history for her and her family. That afternoon when she did not arrive home at her normal time, her mother called the school to inquire about her daughter. She was informed Natascha had never arrived that morning.

The authorities searched for days for Natascha, and days turned into weeks. After many years of searching, they felt she must have been killed. They told her mother to face that fact and mourn the death of her daughter. However, her mother refused to accept that as a fact and continued to hold out hope she would be found. Natascha Maria chose not to fall into despair but to hold onto positive thoughts for her daughter.

Amazingly enough, Natacha's mother was right. Her daughter was alive! She had been abducted, physically abused, and held in a cellar made of concrete walls by her kidnapper, Wolfgang Přiklopil, for years. Over time, he allowed her to come out of the dark, dank cellar to cook and clean for him. As time went on, he began to take her out with him in public. He threatened her and said he would kill anyone she spoke to. She was too scared to try to run away, and for more than eight years she was his captive.

One day he gave her the job of vacuuming his van. Unlike all the other times, he forgot to lock the exterior gate that surrounded the yard, and it was slightly open. His cell phone rang, and he picked it up to answer. Since he couldn't hear over the noise of the vacuum, he had to walk away to finish his conversation. When he walked away from her view, she saw her opportunity to escape. On August 23, 2006, she slipped through the unlocked gate, and finally gained her freedom after eight and a half long, lonely, terror-filled, and abusive years.

As I heard Natascha relate how she made it through, I was amazed at the wisdom she exhibited which far surpassed her years. She was kidnapped at the age of ten and found freedom at the age of eighteen.

When they asked her how she managed, mentally, to survive, her response was one of the healthiest I had ever heard. She said she realized her captor could keep her locked away, starve her to death, force her to do heavy labor, but he could *never* touch her mind unless she allowed it. She was in control of her thoughts.

She also realized that if she hated him, it would destroy her, not him, so for her own sake, she stated she forgave him almost immediately after he committed any offense against her. She was determined he would not affect her mind, and when she was free of the physical jail he created, she needed to emotionally be free, as well. She realized Wolfgang had an issue with his mind which contributed to his rationale for kidnaping her, controlling, and dominating her.

I don't know about you, but I am not sure if I would have come out with such a mentally healthy attitude. Natascha made a choice. She could have caved in and let her circumstances suck her into darkness. But she chose to maintain a positive attitude in the midst of a seemingly hopeless situation.

When we choose to first mourn, let the pain and heartache go, trust in God like a child, and ask for the grace to truly forgive ourselves and others from the depths of our souls, then we control the outcome of our minds. Below are some words that emphasize positive thinking. Remember, God never tells us to do anything that is counterproductive, so we have to trust His way is best. We have to push past the fleshly desire to give in to despair and grab hold of the Word of God. That is how we will draw strength when we think we just can't make it one more day.

"Why art thou cast down, O my soul? and why art thou disquieted within me? hope thou in God: for I shall yet praise him, who is the health of my countenance, and my God" (Psalm 42:11).

"In God I will praise his word, in God I have put my trust; I will not fear what flesh can do unto me" (Psalm 56:4).

Handling Regret And Overcoming Depression

"My heart is fixed, O God, my heart is fixed: I will sing and give praise" (Psalm 57:7).

Find ways to laugh

Laughter is great way to get out of the pit!

One Sunday in church, I heard the story of Norman Cousins who used the power of the mind for healing. I was fascinated by the man's methods and wanted to know the whole story. I found the rest of the story on the Internet (laughofflife).

> "Hearty laugher is a good way to jog internally without having to go outdoors." Norman Cousins.

Norman Cousins wrote an autobiography entitled, *Anatomy of an Illness*. Cousins tells of a difficult time in his life and describes how he recovered from ankylosing spondylitis. This disease is "a painful collagen illness that rendered him immobile, and at its nadir, nearly incapable of moving his jaw." Apparently, the odds of fully recovering from this disease were exceptionally low; only one in 500 had a chance for full recovery. Cousins was not one to sit around having a pity party, so he researched the causes that triggered this disease and learned the options for healing.

"Relying on previously read books on the subject, such as Hans Selye's *The Stress of Life*, he learned that negative emotions, such as frustration or suppressed rage, are linked to adrenal exhaustion.

Therefore, Cousins assumed the opposite to be true, that positive emotions—love, hope, faith, laughter, confidence—would yield salutary results."

He found there were two remedies that could be used to help the healing process. The first remedy was high doses of Vitamin C. He learned the immune system needed to be repaired to reduce inflammation and to build up his adrenal glands.

Here is where the story gets interesting. He found a second unusual remedy—one pharmacist wish they could bottle and sell-laughter. Yes, that is correct! He watched and listened to anything and everything that would make him laugh. Daily, he set aside time to laugh. He watched the Marx Brothers films, *Candid Camera*, and selections from E.B. White's *Subtreasury of American Humor*. He found that after just ten minutes of enthusiastic, robust laughter he could acquire pain-free moments and said he even got two hours of uninterrupted sleep. Isn't that amazing?

After several years, the results from his unorthodox self-treatment yielded little to no pain in day-to-day living. "Though he relied on Vitamin C to physically repair his immune system, he relied on the often-overlooked medication of laughter to mentally cure his condition and live to the age of 75."

Norman chose to use a well-known but often overlooked biblical principle found in the book of Proverbs, as expressed in these verses:

Handling Regret And Overcoming Depression

"A merry heart doeth good like a medicine: but a broken spirit drieth the bones" (Proverbs 17:22).

"A merry heart maketh a cheerful countenance: but by sorrow of the heart, the spirit is broken" (Proverbs 15:13).

Norman Cousins applied the principle that a happy attitude can fix a broken body. He chose to let his mind focus on positive thoughts which led to positive actions, followed by positive habits that finally gave him positive results.

Find community

During this journey of healing, God brought people into my life or led me to programs and Bible studies that helped me tremendously. One such program was called DivorceCare. "DivorceCare is a friendly, caring group of people who will walk alongside you through one of life's most difficult experiences" (divorcecare.org).

DivorceCare groups are all over the country. You can check out this website for one near you: https://www.divorcecare.org/findagroup.

At the DivorceCare meeting, I met several people who became my friends. We stay in touch, get together periodically on the weekends or during holidays, group text words of encouragement, Scripture, comical moments, and jokes.

Finding community can lead to new friendships that can help incorporate Norman Cousins' therapy of laughter.

Through the DivorceCare Group, I met a woman named Fran. Fran and I are partners in crime when it comes to belly-rolling laughter. Have you ever laughed so hard you almost peed your pants? You may snort in derision, thinking to yourself you don't have anything to laugh about, but I am here to tell you that, one day, that feeling will go away and you will laugh again. Whenever Fran and I get together, we find anything and everything to laugh about. Half the time we start laughing and don't even know why we are laughing. It's truly therapeutic!

Many times, over the past couple of years, I had a lot of what I call "blonde moments." Those are moments when I do things that are a little ditzy. I have even nicknamed myself Lucy after Lucille Ball of the "I Love Lucy Show." When I was building new healthy habits, I took those silly "Lucy" moments to share with others so we could laugh together. Since I want to help you laugh again, I am going to share some of those ditzy moments.

In my profession of being a Realtor®, I am on the phone all the time, constantly emailing, texting, or calling. I get very tired of using my index finger to type out my text messages. I know, don't laugh, I cannot text with my two thumbs, so I peck away at the keyboard. When I get tired of pecking, I "Siri talk" my messages.

I am a stickler for spelling out my words and using punctuation. I am not going to give in and stop using periods, exclamation points, and questions marks. I learned a little trick, when Siri is talking you can say "question mark" and it will incorporate a ? symbol.

So one day, I called my assistant, Amber, who is also my very good friend and left a message. It went something like this:

"Hello, I am running errands. I will be at the office at 2 p.m. Will you be there question mark.........OH MY GOODNESS! Did I really SAY question mark when leaving a VOICEMAIL????? I am totally losing it!" (bursts of uncontrollable laughter as I spit out the last sentence).

We laughed about that for days. Use those moments! Capitalize on them. When you are going through a disruptive event like a separation or a divorce, your mind is going a million miles, and it's very hard to focus. Shoot, I locked myself out of the house so many times in the course of six months I broke out one of my real estate lockboxes and put it on my house. Best decision I ever made during that time. I am chuckling over the memory. It sounds silly, but it worked for me. I laughed at myself every time I had to use it too.

Or, how about the time I was talking on the phone to a friend. I began gathering my things so I could run to the office and then hit the road for the rest of the day: computer, computer bag, lunch, water bottle, purse, phone. PHONE...WHERE IS MY PHONE? Panic set in as I began to run through the house looking for it. My friend on the other end of the phone stuttered out a tentative, "Uh, you have a house phone? I thought I called your cell phone." Silence from me.... quickly processing two options: *Do I own up to the fact I am indeed on my cell phone, or can I pretend for just a moment that I have a landline?* My laughter came rolling out, and I started laughing so hard I was afraid I might really pee my pants this time for real!

Oh my, remembering all those "blonde moments" may have you questioning my sanity. That's okay, for at times, I too question my sanity. I really hope I made you laugh, and I really hope you won't be too hard on yourself when you have your own comical moments. We all have them, but as my mom likes to say, "This too shall pass."

Laugh. Laugh at yourself. Share your laughter with others. There is always someone going through something harder than what you are dealing with. Be an encouragement to them whether it is just being goofy or sharing a joke. That encouragement you give will come back around and help lift you from being dejected to joyous.

Take care of yourself physically.

The Lord created us as physical, emotional, mental, and spiritual beings. All aspects of our mind and body are connected. I found if I could get myself moving, my thoughts would start heading in a more positive direction.

When my husband walked out the door, I had this nervous energy. I literally could not stay focused on a thought or sit still for more than five minutes. There was a driving force inside of me to move. I began walking every day, multiple times a day. I began walking almost five miles every day. I walked, prayed, cried, listened to encouraging messages and songs, or called a friend. It helped me tremendously.

(Silver lining: I lost weight with all the exercise and healthy eating. I couldn't stomach more than a protein shake a couple times a day and vegetables, so naturally I lost weight. I was the healthiest I had been in years.)

I later found out the reason I was feeling better physically was, in part, due to all the exercise. Exercise releases endorphins. Research explains, "These endorphins interact with the receptors in your brain that reduce your perception of pain. Endorphins also trigger a positive feeling in the body, similar to that of morphine. Many studies show that people who exercise regularly benefit with a positive boost in mood and lower rates of depression" (webmd.com).

Give it a try, if you haven't been getting exercise, at least force yourself to walk around the block or buy a mini trampoline and jump on it in the privacy of your home. Ask God for guidance. Yes, He cares about even what type of exercise you do so you don't hurt yourself. Ask–God will help.

Applying the Principles

I pray for peace and success as you apply these guidelines for avoiding regretful actions and techniques to combat depression.

As you lean into Jesus, let Him take away the regrets and depression. Let Him heal your soul. Give those negative thoughts the ole "kick in the pants" and send them down the road.

Praise the Lord for His goodness and provision, as promised in this verse, *"And the LORD, he it is that doth go before thee; he will be with thee, he will not fail thee, neither forsake thee: fear not, neither be dismayed"* (Deuteronomy 31:8).

We serve an amazing God. We know it is always the darkest before the dawn. Give Him praise and watch the storm clouds roll away, as the light of day begins to break through. The sun will shine again, life will take on new meaning, and your purpose will be made known.

HEALING TOOLS:

Memorize Scripture: *"In whom we have redemption through his blood, the forgiveness of sins, according to the riches of his grace"* (Ephesians 1:7).

"Thou wilt keep him in perfect peace, whose mind is stayed on thee: because he trusteth in thee" (Isaiah 26:3).

Meditate on the Journal of Psalms:

(A Psalm of David, when he was in the wilderness of Judah.)

Handling Regret And Overcoming Depression

"O God, thou art my God; early will I seek thee: my soul thirsteth for thee, my flesh longeth for thee in a dry and thirsty land, where no water is;
To see thy power and thy glory, so as I have seen thee in the sanctuary.
Because thy lovingkindness is better than life, my lips shall praise thee.
Thus will I bless thee while I live: I will lift up my hands in thy name. My soul shall be satisfied as with marrow and fatness; and my mouth shall praise thee with joyful lips:
When I remember thee upon my bed, and meditate on thee in the night watches.
Because thou hast been my help, therefore in the shadow of thy wings will I rejoice.
My soul followeth hard after thee: thy right hand upholdeth me" (Psalm 63:1-8).

Praise Often and Daily: Lord, I praise You because You love me even when I am weak. I praise You for the peace that keeps my heart and mind so much so that it passes all understanding.

Prayer Decree: Lord, help me to take into captivity every thought so my mind lines up with Yours. I know the truth is what will set me free, and I choose to keep that truth in front of me, guarding my heart and mind with the truth of Your love.

Focused Thought: Fear is from the enemy. I have been given a spirit of love, power, and of a sound mind along with laughter… it's darn good medicine.

Lesson 7

Overcoming Rejection, Bitterness, and UnForgiveness

Being Real

I'm going to be completely honest. This chapter is the most open, honest, and raw chapter in the whole book. I debated whether to be so "real" by adding my journal entries or just skip them. I have gone back and read through my journal entries from those early days of separation, and as I read, I cringed. Those entries are filled with totally unfiltered emotions I was going through at the time. I see bitterness seeping through, along with hurt, rejection, and feelings of worthlessness. All those shattered feelings were a part of a broken marriage.

Those emotions needed to come out, and it was imperative I deal with them. All that garbage needed to be spoken, acknowledged, and laid at the foot of the cross. It is a part of the healing process. Dealing with the break-up of a marriage or a relationship feels like the worst form of rejection.

The broken marriage and the accompanying hurt feelings cut deeply because that other person is walking away from you. Rejection tears at the core of who you are. It is the tearing apart of two people who had become one. If we rip or cut a part of our flesh, we know certain things need to happen for healing to take place. There is a process, a right way and a wrong way, to deal with the torn flesh. The tear may get infected and need extra attention. At times, peroxide might need to be poured over the infected spot. That will cause more temporary pain, but it will cleanse the wound and bring healing more quickly.

I found that when I acknowledged my pain, talked about it, and brought it to Jesus, it was a bit like pouring peroxide over a wound. It was painful to acknowledge both my faults and the faults of others who wounded me, but so necessary to the process of healing.

What a mouthful—rejection, bitterness, and unforgiveness. I dealt with many emotions, like anger, pride, rage, loneliness, betrayal, and more, while going through my separation, but the toughest of all was sorting through rejection, bitterness, and the choice to forgive or not! I discovered being rejected can lead to hurt, and hurt, when forgiveness is not extended, can lead to bitterness. I had to quickly figure out a way to sort through all those emotions. I had to either let go of rejection and bitterness or embrace forgiveness, but I could not do both.

Overcoming Rejection, Bitterness, And Unforgiveness

Rejection

Feelings of rejection, of being cast off and snubbed, can seep into every part of our minds—if we allow. Dealing with the feelings of being rejected was not an immediate response at the beginning of the separation. It took a while for me to process that feeling of rejection, so it just sat there under the surface. The wound was there but didn't manifest itself until almost a year later after the divorce was finalized.

During the second year following our separation, I battled with getting my feelings hurt and then having overwhelming feelings of rejection overtake me. It seemed like something would happen, I'd get my feelings hurt, and then I'd eventually work through it. I would think, "Wow, I'm glad that's over; now I surely must have dealt with all those thoughts of rejection." Then another situation and scenario would arise, triggering the rejection wound, and I would find myself going through all the same emotions again.

I had to deal with the rejection in multiple facets and on different levels. There was the rejection from my husband in choosing another woman while we were still married, and then purposefully walking away. There was rejection from family members. As time went on, I felt like I was being rejected by friends, church family, and co-workers. The thing was I very rarely got offended or hurt in the past, so I began to analyze my feelings and ask myself why I was feeling so hurt all the time. I slowly understood that I was being triggered by past hurts. I began to consider that perhaps all the rejection I was feeling from those around me was not valid. I came to understand that some of it was true rejection while parts of those rejected feelings were made up in my wounded mind, in my shattered soul.

The spirit of rejection is one of the hardest battles to overcome! Here is the thing—we can't just ask God to take the spirit of rejection from us and expect this removal to happen all at once. Nor can we pray a prayer of forgiveness for someone and expect never to have to repeat the prayer. The reason is that deep issues like rejection come in layers, like an onion, as we discussed in a previous lesson. What we have to do with the emotions of being shunned and rejected is deal with one "onion ring" at a time, as they occur. I became aware of those "onion rings" through triggers. We all have triggers; some are similar, and others are extremely unique.

Triggers

I mentioned triggers in a previous chapter but want to delve a little more into this. What is a trigger? I think a trigger is something that activates you or causes you to have a memory. That memory prompts a strong emotion which usually causes a response. The *Merriam-Webster Dictionary* definition is "to cause an intense and usually negative emotional reaction in (someone.)"

For instance, if you are watching a movie and you see one of the main characters cheating on the other, this infidelity may elicit a response deep within you, causing emotions to bubble up. You

Overcoming Rejection, Bitterness, And Unforgiveness

may have a negative feeling towards the actor or actress playing the part come over you. Another trigger could be getting a letter notifying you of a pending court date or possibly a notification in the mail stating you are no longer on your spouse's health insurance policy. Those are all triggers. Those triggers cause an emotional reaction inside. Below is a journal entry from a day where several events happened that triggered my pain and fears:

Journal:

---------❋---------

"I am heartbroken. I went through such despair this morning, sobbing my eyes out, with my husband being unwilling to help me on any level. He wants to talk about expenses and dividing up all the finances. I vacillate from despair to anger surrendering to God. When he talks of dividing everything up, it's as if he has given up on our marriage for good, and then I fall into despair. When he doesn't want to help or talk, I get so angry.

"I feel like I am a failure. Within two months my life has been torn to pieces, and everything I believed to be true is now being tested. My husband, whom I love, doesn't love me. The kids, whom I have fought to protect, have trained to serve and love God, seem not to care. Those around me that I would have expected support from have vanished. It is as if the past 10 years haven't even existed. How is it possible for some family members to be so calloused and uncaring? Is there no connection or bond at all? I am so hurt. Shattered. Devastated. All these past years of trying so hard to honor God, raise the kids right, be fair, love all the children the best I can, respect my husband, go over and above to meet the needs of all. Has it all been for nothing? Or have I just been such a complete and utter failure across the board? Two men who had

promised to love me FOREVER have left me. WHY? What have I done? Am I being punished? What is wrong with me that I can be so easily discarded like trash?"

See the triggers? My husband wanted to divide up the finances. What was once one was now two. He gave no indication he wanted to work on the marriage which was my heart's desire—another trigger. My children had withdrawn, triggering thoughts that I wasn't a good enough mother. Multiple triggers caused me to spin downward.

Once I realized I was heading into a downward spiral, acknowledging I had been triggered, I would talk myself off the ledge of self-doubts and put-downs. My goal was not to react until I processed the trigger, my initial reaction, and possible reasons for my emotions. I had to ask God for clarity.

For instance, when I felt like a failure as a mother and felt my children didn't care anymore, I understood I was being triggered. Therefore, all the thoughts that followed were not actually logical but emotional. My children really *did* care; they just didn't know what to say or do. They still loved me. My feeling of rejection had nothing to do with them at all. Those emotions came because of my wounds, and I just needed to shift my perspective.

Emotional triggers can lead us down a dark hole filled with feelings of despair, depression, and rejection. I believe rejection, when not dealt with, can lead to bitterness.

Bitterness

I was on the path to becoming a bitter woman. Here is another very raw and angry journal entry:

Journal:

---❋---

"I am very angry at my mother-in-law. How can she support her son when he is clearly going against the Word of God? There are no biblical grounds for him to leave our marriage, yet she is supporting his decision. She has been teaching the Word of God for almost 50 years. She has been to Bible college and has a Bible degree. Where is all that righteous anger against sin I have seen her display over the years? I am angry at my husband. I have been praying and praying for both to see the error of their ways, but also, I have been praying God will protect them and bless them. Now, I have had enough! I just can't pray God will bless them anymore! I don't want them to be blessed. I want them to suffer the consequences of their sin. I am very angry, and I do not understand how godly Christians can do something so wrong. God, You are going to have to help me because I can't seem to get a grip on this frustration and anger."

---❋---

God was working on my heart to gently show me I was becoming bitter. I did not want that. He brought this verse to my attention, *"Looking diligently lest any man fail of the grace of God; lest any root of bitterness springing up trouble you, and thereby many be defiled"* (Hebrews 12:15).

Shortly after God highlighted that verse, I was listening to a message online and heard a story of how bitterness does not bring healing but further contamination.

Story of Joab and Abner: The Bite of Bitterness

> "Sin will take you farther than you want to go, keep you longer than you want to stay, and cost you more than you want to pay."
> —Ravi Zacharias

In the story of Joab and Abner we see depicted the truth of those words spoken by Ravi Zacharias. Outlined below are the details showing how the seeds of hurt and pain turn into bitterness that wreaks havoc on the lives of those who feed and water those seeds.

The setting of this story takes place during wartime, approximately 1005 BC, and is a tale of two men named Joab and Abner. Joab is the general for Judah whose king is David. Abner is the general for Israel who just lost Saul as king. It's a story of two generals, two sides, and a five-year feud which began and ended in tragedy.

Let me recap the story found in 2 Samuel 2. General Joab and his two brothers, Asahel and Abishai, were out doing their typical reconnaissance when they unexpectedly found themselves face-to-face with the opposing army led by General Abner.

As they came to a standstill, staring each other down across a body of water, Abner came up with an idea. He suggested rather than have the whole army engage in a lengthy and devastating battle, they should each send twelve men to fight to the death. Basically, it was a situation where the last man standing would win. As they battled it out, an unexpected outcome occurred. Each man killed the other, and all 24 men fell down dead. Neither side won. In this scenario, I would say that was a given. It was a lose-lose proposition from the start.

When all 24 men died, pandemonium erupted, causing Judah and Israel's short- lived truce to come to a screeching halt. It was now "game on." Since no level-headed person seemed to be in sight, the soldiers engaged in hand-to-hand combat as they had been trained to do. Those testosterone-filled men began to fight in earnest, no holds barred.

As the battle progressed, it was becoming apparent that Israel, led by Abner, was losing the fight. The army of Israel saw their general Abner take off at a run for the hills. That was the sign to retreat, and Israel began to fall back.

Asahel, Joab's brother, saw what was happening and decided to run after Abner. Remember, Asahel just saw twelve of their best men die. The best of the best surrounded Joab, Asahel, and Abishai, I would imagine that since they depended on one another to guard their backs, in a life and death situation, it strengthened their bond significantly. Asahel must have been very good friends with several of those who had just died.

Wanting to get revenge for the death of his friends, Asahel was hot under the collar and was not about to let the man responsible for all the bloodshed get away. Asahel was an extremely fast runner and was known throughout the region for his speed. He took off after Abner like an Olympian sprinter. Abner heard a soldier coming after him, and due to the speed of the soldier, he guessed it was Asahel.

Abner was confident he would be able to kill Asahel, but he didn't want to. Asahel was closing in on Abner, and Abner called out to him, telling him to get one of the other soldier's armor. Abner wanted Asahel to put on some armor so when they entered hand-to-hand combat, he would not be fatally wounded. That seems counterproductive to me. Each army was intent on fighting to kill, but Abner did not want to kill the general's brother.

Joab was known for his ability to "get even," and he was also known as one who would take things into his own hands to get a job done. Abner knew he would be a dead man if he killed Joab's brother. He tried again to persuade hot-headed Asahel to stop chasing him, but he would not. Abner had to decide at that point— kill or be killed.

Abner killed Asahel.

Joab and Abishai finally caught up to Asahel in time to find him dead on the ground. The two brothers and their army pursued Abner. At nightfall, exhausted, they finally caught up with Abner. Abner saw them and surmised their intent to keep the battle going. Abner was doing what he did best in a battle as a general: he

Overcoming Rejection, Bitterness, And Unforgiveness

weighed the situation and came up with a solution. He presented a valid argument.

In 2 Samuel 2:26 we read, *"Then Abner called to Joab, and said, 'Shall the sword devour for ever? knowest thou not that it will be bitterness in the latter end? How long shall it be then, ere thou bid the people return from following their brethren?'"*

Abner made it very clear that to continue the fighting would cause "bitterness in the latter end." Joab apparently was very aware of the consequence of allowing bitterness to continue. He gave in to Abner. He called off his army, and they all went on about their business.

The story continues in 2 Samuel 2:27-28: *"And Joab said, 'As God liveth, unless thou hadst spoken, surely then in the morning the people had gone up everyone from following his brother.' So, Joab blew a trumpet, and all the people stood still, and pursued after Israel no more, neither fought they any more."*

Fast forward about five years later. King David wanted to make peace with Abner and wanted him to serve under him. Abner, disenchanted with the current king, agreed. While this alliance was happening, Joab was out fighting another battle. When he came home, he was given an update on the newly created truce.

Joab confronted King David. In 2 Samuel 3:24b- 25b, Joab says," *"'What hast thou done? ... Thou knowest Abner the son of Ner, that he came to deceive thee, and to know thy going out and thy coming in, and to know all that thou doest.'"*

Joab was beside himself that the king had made peace with Abner. It seemed even though on that day, five years before, he had backed down and walked away, he had kept the hatred and bitterness alive in his soul. Joab gave his argument to King David, but the Bible passage in 2 Samuel 3:20-30 doesn't say David responded or backed down from his decision.

We see Joab, whip into a fury, leave the king, and take matters into his hands. He ordered a messenger to track down Abner and bring him to Hebron. Joab's intentions were not of peace but of death.

In 2 Samuel 3:27 we see his intentions, *"And when Abner was returned to Hebron, Joab took him aside in the gate to speak with him quietly, and smote him there under the fifth rib, that he died, for the blood of Asahel his brother."* And in verse 30 we read, *"So Joab and Abishai his brother slew Abner, because he had slain their brother Asahel at Gibeon in the battle."*

The seed of bitterness brought about death. Not only did it affect Abner, Joab, and his brother Asahel, but this bitterness also affected Joab's family for generations. When King David heard about Abner's death, he quickly stated he did not order his death, and he wanted to have nothing to do with it. *"And afterward when David heard it, he said, 'I and my kingdom are guiltless before the LORD for ever from the blood of Abner the son of Ner'"* (2 Samuel 3:28).

Overcoming Rejection, Bitterness, And Unforgiveness

Apparently, back in Abner and Joab's time, it was well known what could come on a family if they allowed bitterness free reign. David and all Israel knew bitterness caused actions that would bring sorrow for generations to come. Consequently, David issued a decree: *"'Let it rest on the head of Joab, and on all his father's house; and let there not fail from the house of Joab one that hath an issue, or that is a leper, or that leaneth on a staff, or that falleth on the sword, or that lacketh bread'"* (2 Samuel 3:29-30).

2 Samuel 3:29 lists the consequences of the sin from feeding bitterness. This was spoken over not just Joab and his brother but on the entire family for generations to come. We see five terrible consequences:

An issue – a sexual discharge
Leprosy
Constant need to walk with a crutch; weakness
Death by sword
Poor and destitute

Goodness! Was getting revenge and taking a life worth it? Do you think the day Joab walked away from that hill he could have even imagined what his life was going to be like in five years' time? He became so bitter when he chose not to forgive that it ate him up inside, and it also had the same effect on his brother. Look at 2 Samuel 3:30. It says that Joab AND Abishai slew Abner.

So how did he end up killing a man, clearly not on the battlefield but secretly? It all started with bitterness. Because he allowed bitterness to simmer and stew like a pot on a stove, his life, and that of his entire family for generations to come, dealt with the consequences in some form of the five points above. Was it worth it?

Here is the irony: the very argument Abner used to get Joab to back down and see reason five years earlier was the same argument he was unable to see due to the fog of bitterness that descended and seeped into his soul until all other solid reasoning was obscured.

We all have a choice, just like Joab did. We can choose to release the vengeance back into God's hands or take it into our own. When we take vengeance into our own hands, we risk major life-changing consequences that will follow not only ourselves but our families as well. I decided to choose forgiveness over bitterness. I wanted health and life over disease and death. I wanted that for myself and for my children.

The way I overcame the pain and heartache of rejection, the rebuffing of who I was and what I had to offer was to delve deeply into who I was in Jesus Christ. Here is a prayer from my journal months into the separation. I give God all the glory and honor for the change He worked in me. Without Him, I would be nothing. I pray the same healing journey will occur in your life as you allow God to heal the wounds of your soul.

Overcoming Rejection, Bitterness, And Unforgiveness

Journal:

---※---

"God, how honored I am to be called Your daughter. I thank You so much for watching out for me and providing for me in ways I never thought possible. You have provided for me financially but more importantly emotionally and spiritually. I have learned to depend on You and to totally trust You (in that arena without boundaries). It is so hard, but I am clinging to faith in Jesus Christ. I am claiming the promises You have given us in Your word that if I ask anything, in Your name, believing, I will receive. So now Lord, I am asking for my marriage to be restored, not the same way, but better with YOU at the front. I am still hoping for reconciliation."

"I am asking that my children AND my husband can bring their problems to You, ask You to heal their wounds and ask each other for forgiveness. Oh God, I know true peace can't come until that happens. Lord, You can change the heart, You know what they need to draw closer to You, to submit their will to Yours, and seek forgiveness and restitution. Lord, show me how I have hurt my children; give me the grace and strength to make it right with them. I want to have a wonderful relationship with them. Help me not to be happy with the "status quo." I don't know how to do that, but God I know You will guide me along the way. Give me clarity and a vision for what I need to do and when. I trust You with my life, my husband, and my seven children. God, put us back together as a family that we might serve you. "Broken together" as the Casting Crowns song says. Help us to be broken together, understanding we are not perfect, but through You we can put the pieces back together.

---※---

Forgiveness

I made a conscious decision to reject a life of bitterness. Now the question became, "How do I truly forgive?" I prayed for God to reveal how to honestly forgive.

One year after my husband walked out the door, I had a dream. In this vivid dream, I saw him coming home. He was walking up the sidewalk with a look of shame and sadness etched on his face. I was standing on the front porch. In this vision as he walked closer, I cried out, "God, help? What am I supposed to say? What am I supposed to do?" My thoughts became a jumble of emotions as I thought of everything I wanted to say; words that would either tear him down or words that would heal the breach."

I instantly saw myself making a choice. I chose to forgive. As I stood there waiting for him, I saw myself slowly extend my arms, reaching out. Arms that reached out in love and mercy, arms willing to accept him just as he was. I wrapped my arms around him and just held him—no words, no anger, no bitterness. Just an understanding that while, yes, many sins had been committed by both sides, there would be no healing or restoration unless forgiveness was first extended. So many things communicated in that one moment, in that one gesture.

I woke up pondering that dream. Honestly, I thought God was showing me my husband would come home, but that did not happen. He married his old high school girlfriend days after our divorce was finalized. Weeks after our divorce when I was talking to God, I asked Him why I had that dream. What was the point?

You see, I doubted my ability to think clearly and my ability of discernment. I needed to understand if I was really hearing God's voice or not. God revealed the vision was for me. I needed to see that act played out. I needed to see and feel that moment when I truly surrendered all my "rights" of anger and bitterness at being the victim. I was surrendering all that vengeance in my heart to God.

God was going to take care of my ex-husband, the woman who chose to commit adultery with him, and my mother-in-law. I just needed to be willing to extend forgiveness in my heart and be prepared for someday when it was requested of me. The day I had that vision was another defining moment towards the path of complete soul healing. One of many moments, many "onion" layers.

You may be wondering how I got to that point and how you can personally get to that same place. I had to constantly remember that vengeance comes from God and He is a righteous judge. He knows what each person needs, who needs grace and mercy, and when to extend those gifts. I got to that moment through months of reading God's Word, digging deeply, and asking Him to show me how to truly forgive. I share my innermost thoughts hoping you too can open your arms wide and step into the healing power of forgiveness.

I asked God to help me FEEL compassion, really feel it for others. I asked Him to help me forgive. God answered my prayers in an odd way. He took me down memory lane where I recalled a moment in my life that was not the most stellar moment I ever had. He recalled to my mind a time I had done wrong and was so ashamed. Can you think of a time when you acted poorly? Where you said or did something inappropriate? Then you will understand how memories of those events can roll through your mind like an action film playing on a large TV screen.

I thought of another time where I was arrogant, prideful, self-righteous, and cocky. As those memories were playing on the screen of my mind, I had a vision of my prideful self, sauntering around strutting like a peacock at the foot of Mount Calvary. That hill where Jesus was hanging on a cross, beaten beyond recognition for me, for my old, sinful self. How did I repay Him? By spitting on and judging those He created and so willingly died for? Those who had hurt me were His creation too. He loved them and died for them just as He did for me.

It is easy to pray and ask for forgiveness and healing for someone you love very much, loveable people like our children and close family members, but what about those who are not so loveable? Many do not have the ability to come to Christ by themselves. They are like wounded soldiers in the ditch.

I want to take a moment and think back to Lesson Two where we saw the example of the woman with the issue of blood, the centurion, and the nobleman. They cried out to Jesus (as we do in prayer), and they each asked for help and healing. Out of those three healings, two of the individuals were unable to come to Jesus themselves. Someone else approached Him for them, stood in the gap with total faith, and sought healing for their loved one. Isn't that what Jesus did?

So now I ask the question, what about that spouse who cheats on you? What about that spouse who is addicted to drugs, alcohol, or pornography? What about that lazy spouse or ex? Who will seek God's assistance for that spouse's healing, if not you? Christ died for us while we were sinners. If we were forgiven while we were still in the midst of our sin, shouldn't we forgive others while they are caught in the snares of theirs? The world will tell you no, but what does God say? Remember, you must *"choose you this day whom you will serve"* (Joshua 24:15). That is not an easy thing to do. Praying with great faith is needed to step into that level of forgiveness. I know that truth, oh so well!

Can you think of ONE person right now with whom you are very angry, but whom you love very much? Maybe they have done something very wrong against themselves or against you. How do you treat them? How do they treat you? In a perfect world, what would you like to have happen? I would venture a guess that if I was personally speaking with you, you would say you want them to love you, treat you respectfully, and for them to do the right thing. Correct?

Maybe you pray for a day when they will come to their senses and realize what they have done. You imagine that person coming to you, apologizing, giving you a hug, and making things right. You wonder when that will be, what that will look like, and maybe you even fantasize about your reply, good or bad!

Okay, now hold that thought.

Now it is time for you to step into your prayer closet and pray for that person. You might ask, how can I pray for one who has wronged me? Let's say it is your spouse, and they have sinned against you, they have betrayed you, or they are just mean and nasty across the board. As you begin to pray, you find you cannot pray for God to bless them anymore because you feel like they should be "punished." Whatever they have done, they deserve everything coming to them. Right?

They should have to suffer for what they have done! You will have many people back you up, validate you, and agree with you.

I am going to challenge your thinking, and I am going to make a statement you will probably think is absolutely crazy. You must pray for God's goodness and blessings. Why? Did you know God's Word says that the goodness of God leads to repentance? Romans 2:4 tells us this truth: *"Or despisest thou the riches of his goodness and forbearance and longsuffering; not knowing that the goodness of God leadeth thee to repentance?"*

If we want that person to be kind, loving, and repentant, we must pray for God's goodness to fall on them. What happens when God's goodness fills someone's life? Romans 2:4 promises that His goodness will cause people to repent and with repentance comes

Overcoming Rejection, Bitterness, And Unforgiveness

change. God's spirit will fill their life, and they will begin to exhibit the fruit of the Spirit.

Without God's goodness we see these qualities (taken from Galatians 5:19-21)

Adultery
Witchcraft
Hatred
Wrath
Strife
Heresies

Drunkenness

This is the list of what happens when God's goodness takes root: (taken from Galatians 5:22-23):

Love
Joy
Peace
Longsuffering
Gentleness
Goodness
Faith
Meekness
Temperance

I am going to guess you would LOVE for the second list to overflow from that person. I want to see the second list demonstrated.

I want to exhibit these qualities, I want my children to live them, and I want others to show them!

How are we able to live like that? How can the second list be made manifest in our lives and in the lives of others? Apostle Paul says in Romans that we, as Christians, are *full of goodness* once we have been filled by God through the power of the Holy Ghost.

"Now the God of hope fill you with all joy and peace in believing, that ye may abound in hope, through the power of the Holy Ghost. And I myself also am persuaded of you, my brethren, that ye also are full of goodness, filled with all knowledge, able also to admonish one another" (Romans 15:13-14).

Once we ask for the filling of God to be in our lives, we are filled with joy and peace because of the *dunamis* power of the Holy Spirit that lives within us. Then we can fully walk in the Fruit of the Spirit. We can pray for others to be filled with the Spirit and that they will walk in the Fruit of the Spirit.

We are commanded to turn the other cheek, (Matthew 5:39) and *"Bless them that curse you, and pray for them which despitefully use you"* (Luke 6:28).

God knows what can happen when we apply these teachings. Our prayers reach the throne room of God and action is taken. The spiritual world is activated on behalf of that person. This is what it means to bear one another's burdens (Galatians 6:2). When they can't pray for themselves because sin has blinded them, WE pray for them. We intercede on their behalf, and we ask God to extend

His hand of mercy and show grace until they can "come to themselves" like the Prodigal Son. It is a GOOD thing for someone to repent—for them and you!

What if you don't see a change in that person? You pray and pray but nothing happens? I struggled with this question for months and months. At the end of the day, I had to make a decision. I had to decide if I was going to obey God and pray for that other person, or was I going to disobey God? I know everyone has a free will and God allows them to choose. I made a choice to give the outcome to God. I turned over my "director's" hat and surrendered my will to Him. God wants me to obey, even if I don't get my own way. I am to surrender even when I don't see a positive outcome.

Forgiveness Heals

I was watching a movie called *Heaven's Rain* on PureFlix. It gives us a contemporary example of how forgiving someone who has dreadfully wronged you can release the bitterness and pain inside. Forgiveness releases the debt owed the soul and makes way for the spiritual "aloe vera" to bring ultimate healing. Here is the storyline from the movie's website:

"Brooks Douglass and his sister, Leslie, grew up in a home filled with love, compassion, and faith. Their father, Richard, was a leader in the Baptist Church. Their mother, Marilyn, was a woman of faith and talent, turning down a scholarship to the renowned Juilliard School to join Richard in the Brazilian mission field."

"They returned from Brazil back to the states when Brooks was aged 16 and Leslie was 12. Their dad, Richard, became pastor of a large church in Oklahoma City. On October 15, 1979, Brooks opened the door of their modest family home to what he believed was a man in need. The man, a drugged-up drifter, named Glen Ake, was joined by his partner, Steven Hatch. They pulled out guns, tied up the Douglasses, repeatedly assaulted Leslie, shot all four family members, and left them for dead. Richard and Marilyn died at the scene. Brooks and Leslie recovered from their wounds, but their ordeal had just begun."

"Ake and Hatch were caught, tried, and in 1980, sentenced to death. For the next 16 years, however, the suffering rolled on as a legal system protected the rights of the accused while dragging the Douglass children time after time to court to testify and to relive that night."

"The story became national news. But it was continuing bad news for Brooks and Leslie, as they were forced to sell their family home and possessions to pay medical bills. Brooks struggled through high school and college, repeatedly failing out, drinking heavily, and given to bouts of rage. Leslie, once a beauty queen with a beautiful voice, fought to put her life together as she dealt with recurring nightmares and struggled in relationships."

"In a 1986 retrial, Ake was convicted again but received life in prison instead of death. Brooks Douglass became convicted as well, convicted the system must no longer "step over the body of a victim to read the criminal his rights." Brooks earned his law degree, and, at age 27, became the youngest state senator in Oklahoma history where he passed a series of victims' rights bill."

In the process of trying to right a wrong he became consumed with the injustice. As bitterness seeped into his soul, the drinking became more pronounced, and he eventually lost his wife through divorce, because he could not let go and let God take control.

In 1995, on a legislative tour of a state prison, Brooks saw Ake and requested a chance to talk to the man who had destroyed his family. *Heaven's Rain* shares the dramatic result of that meeting.

Brooks Douglas had to decide in his heart if he was going to forgive the men that did this to his family. This movie showed his real-life struggle of letting go of the pain, anger, bitterness, and unforgiveness directed at these men and even at God. At the end of the movie, we see Brooks asking the prison guard to set up a meeting with him and Ake. He was alone with the man who was responsible for killing his parents, raping his sister, and destroying their lives.

This was his opportunity to take all that pent-up anger and animosity out on Ake. It was his chance to beat him to a pulp, to give back just a tiny portion of what Ake doled out. It was a chance to right the wrong and make Brooks feel better by having done something, anything, to exact revenge. In that moment of decision, he could do what he came to do which was to beat him up, or he could, in honor of his father and the Word of God, surrender all those negative thoughts and feelings in one act of forgiveness.

He extended the keys to the handcuffs to Ake, as an act of giving him his forgiveness. With that one act, the burden he carried for all those years rolled off his back. The pain, anguish, hatred, and bitterness—all of it was gone. Sweet relief came in the form of forgiveness that flowed through his heart and mind. He released the debt and gave it to God. At that moment, his life changed.

Freedom came as he released Ake from the prison of his mind. Freedom came with the release of the shackles of those soul wounds. Brooks walked out of the prison that night a freed man. Although he had never been physically locked up. By holding onto the hurt, he had been a prisoner in his mind (*Heaven's Rain* Movie).

Letting Go

I can assure you; this was a challenging chapter to write as I recalled hurts on my journey of forgiveness. As I've written in this lesson, forgiveness is not necessarily a one-time event, but a process. As we continually seek God and His ways, however, we will see results. There will be a day when we desire what God wants more than what we want.

So many promises in Scripture point us to the rewards of following and obeying God. In the verses below, we do not see God promise no heartaches or hardships. It is not a promise that obeying Him will necessarily be an easy or a smooth path. However, God does promise He will be with us, defending us, blessing us as we trust in Him – with every aspect of our lives.

"For a day in thy courts is better than a thousand. I had rather be a doorkeeper in the house of my God, than to dwell in the tents of wickedness. For the LORD God is a sun and shield: the LORD will give grace and glory: no good thing will he withhold from them that walk uprightly. O LORD of hosts, blessed is the man that trusteth in thee" (Psalm 84, 10-12)

HEALING TOOLS:

Memorize Scripture: *"Forbearing one another, and forgiving one another, if any man have a quarrel against any: even as Christ forgave you, so also do ye. ...And let the peace of God rule in your hearts"* (Colossians 3:13-17,15a).

Meditate on the Journal of Psalms: *"Be merciful unto me, O Lord: for I cry unto thee daily...For thou, Lord, art good, and ready to forgive; and plenteous in mercy unto all them that call upon thee"* (Psalm 86:3, 5)

Praise Often and Daily: I praise You, God that while I was in my sin You forgave me, loved me, and made a way for me to be redeemed. I give You praise for Your mercy and grace.

Shattered Souls Made Whole

Prayer Decree: Lord, there is so much rejection causing deep wounds in my soul. Lord, I choose to forgive, let go, and give them to You. Today, I choose to let go and give all that pain, heartache, and bitterness to You. I choose to forgive as Jesus did for me.

Focused Thought: "Sin will take you farther than you want to go, keep you longer than you want to stay, and cost you more than you want to pay." — Ravi Zacharias

I CHOOSE TO LET GO!

Lesson 8

Finding Your Purpose

"What's the point?" Steven asked his children after watching them play a video game on their electronic devices. Pastor Steven Furtick continues telling the story in a message entitled "The Secret Scoreboard," explaining that his children were so entertained by a video game they didn't look up for 30 minutes. He watched them play from a distance and grew intrigued that his kids were so entertained for so long. He decided to investigate what was so exciting. He went behind them so he could see the screen and watched them for a few minutes. He saw them clicking on the cookies and watched them disappear.

He kept watching because he was drawn in to see how it ended. It didn't look like it was going to end anytime soon, so finally he asked, "Do you win something, or, you know, like save the princess or get to be the king of the hill or something? What's the point?"

The kids replied with a bit of impatience, "No, Dad."

Then he asked, "What's the point of getting the cookie?"

You see, in that game as you eliminate cookies, you just kept getting more and more cookies as you raise a level, but you never "win" anything. The concept was foreign to him, and it is to me too. You can tell how old we are by that last statement, right? If I am going to do something, I want to know it has a purpose. I want to help someone or be a part of something great and good.

Why are we here? What is our purpose? Or in the words of Pastor Furtick, "What's the point?" We get up, go to work, run errands, go back home, sleep (blessed sleep) to only repeat the cycle the next day. There must be more than just trying to get as many "cookies" as we can on any given day. There must be more meaning than that. Each one of us is put on this earth for a purpose, to be part of something greater than ourselves. It is not just about "getting the most cookies."

It is my prayer as you read through this final chapter, you will zero in on the specific calling God has for you. Everyone has a distinctive, unique calling. We all have desires, dreams, and gifts which are from God. He will use those to guide you into His will and into His calling. The Bible says God will give you the "desires of your heart," as we see in this verse: "Delight thyself also in the LORD; and he shall give thee the desires of thine heart" (Psalm 37:4). Robert Browning who reminds us that, "Our desires and dreams are nothing compared to God's desires and dreams for our lives." We are children of a Holy Father who wants nothing but the best for us. He knows us better than we know ourselves. God knows exactly what ideas we need to throw out and which we should keep. When we "follow hard" after Him, He will make His will and His calling evident to us.

Questions of Life

What is my purpose now? That may be a question you are asking. When we are married, we have another person to consider and much of our time and energy surrounds that person, along with immediate family. So, what are we supposed to do now?

Life is different. For some of us, the separation or divorce happened suddenly, with little to no warning. For others, the yelling, fighting, and disrespect was a daily occurrence, and the breakup of the marriage was no shocker, yet still difficult. Either way, life is different.

We are no longer a couple. We no longer must consider our spouse's wishes before we make a decision. Those decisions may be as small as turning off the light for early bedtime out of consideration or as big as where to go on the next year's family vacation or which house to buy. When we find ourselves alone a whole new mindset settles in.

I didn't realize how many decisions I made through the lens of another person until my husband was gone. For me, once the shock wore off, I felt at a loss. I didn't know my role anymore. I wasn't a wife. My kids were getting older, becoming independent. I felt my role as mother begin to diminish and shift from the daily hands-on approach to more of a counselor, one who was there when needed. Shifting into the "empty-nester" stage is hard enough without the loss of a spouse. I felt empty and alone, with no sense of purpose, drifting out to sea with no anchor, no oar, no sail to direct me.

I had to find my purpose, my specific calling, again, not as a wife and mother, just as a single person, without being an extension of someone else. I struggled to find meaning and answers to my questions, as you can see in my journal below.

My Journal:

---❋---

"I heard this quote today by Jeff Bridges: 'Obeying God is worked out within well-defined boundaries of God's revealed will. But trusting God is worked out in an arena that has no boundaries.' That is where I am right now. God's revealed will is clear, such as the Ten Commandments: they are black and white. We all know it's wrong to kill someone or steal. We all know God says to "honor your father and mother." We know we are commanded to "love the Lord your God with all your heart, soul and mind." Those items fall under God's revealed will. So, what about God's calling for me, specifically? Walking in the middle of trusting God with everything and in every area of my life feels like my brain is infiltrated with foggy, gray soup. What does God want me to do? Where does He want me to go? Who am I? What is my purpose? I am in the arena of life with no boundaries. Trusting Him, step by step, to show me is the only way to walk safely on this path of life."

---❋---

Our Ultimate Purpose

God's purpose for our lives and His revealed will is spelled out in the following verses:

*"Thou art worthy, O Lord, to receive glory and honour and power: for thou hast created all things, and **for thy pleasure they are and were created**"* (Revelation 4:11).

Our ultimate purpose is found in 2 Thessalonians 1:11. I am going to add in words in brackets to expand on the vocabulary.

"Wherefore also we pray always for you, that our God would count you worthy of this calling, [an invitation] and fulfil all the good pleasure [purpose] of his goodness, and the work of faith [salvation] with power: [miraculous, ability] **That the name of our Lord Jesus Christ may be glorified in you, and ye in him,** *according to the grace of our God and the Lord Jesus Christ."*

Our Calling

As Christians, our sense of purpose comes through our Creator and what He created us for. Our ultimate purpose is defined in the verses above—to bring honor and glory to Him. That is God's revealed will. Yet each one of us has a unique way in which we honor and please God. I will call that specific purpose, "our calling." We have God-given desires from the Creator Himself. He is not going to force a non-detailed person into the role of an accountant.

Or stuff a non-artistic person into a creative role in which he or she would struggle immensely. God created us for a unique purpose, and I believe it will be something we enjoy doing, a desire, or a dream.

So, how can you find out what your unique purpose, your calling, should be? How do I know what mine is? I struggled with those questions for many months. I believe the way in which we bring glory and honor to God changes as our lives change. When we are teenagers, we can relate and honor God in different avenues and venues than when we are 40 years old, or after having children, or after experiencing a death of a loved one. Those events change our lives, and we are then able to redefine our particular calling according to God's will for us at that moment.

Finding God's will…that is a mouthful. Half the time I wonder if anyone really knows what that is. I know I questioned it. It is not like I can open the Bible and go to Valerie 1:1 and see exactly what God wants me to do in this precise moment. Being "in God's will" always seemed ambiguous to me. Finding "God's will" seemed like it was a mystery that only the extremely spiritual people, such as those in the ministry, were able to seek, find, and emphatically state they were "in it." Trusting God to lead me into His will felt a bit like walking in the desert without a compass. Yet I wanted to know, without a doubt. I wanted a formula, a plan to share with my children, family, and friends, so they too could know God's will beyond a shadow of a doubt. I started researching the Scriptures to find a pattern or a path to seeing God's will on an individual basis. What was God's plan for me, at this moment, currently, in my life? And how exactly would I know?

Let me take you back to the time when I was questioning my new role, my calling, now as a single woman, and almost an empty-nester. I began to evaluate my job, my church, my friends, and where I lived. I asked questions, such as, "Why was I working in the field of real estate? If I could wave a magic wand right now and have any job I wanted, what would it be? Was I at the right church? Am I surrounding myself with the right friends?" I examined my past decisions. I questioned my ability of discernment. Everything was up for grabs; my whole life was one big question mark!

For the next several months, I began taking those question marks to God. One by one, I laid out the pros and cons of each during my prayer time and throughout the day as a thought popped into my mind. I would remind myself of James 1:5 which says if anyone needs wisdom, God will give a huge dose of it. All I had to do was ask. So, I asked.

I sought counsel from those in my inner circle. When I asked for help regarding my job, a good friend suggested I play out each decision in my mind and see where it went. For example, I wasn't sure if I should change jobs or stay in the same line of work. He suggested I look at other jobs, see if I could find one that "fit." So, I went online and found a posted job I thought I would like, and I pretended I got the job. I envisioned getting up every morning, going to that new place of work, and being a part of that world, day in and day out. Did it "feel right," did it fit with who I was?

That was great counsel. I did what he said, and after a couple months of wrestling with it and playing out that exercise, I had an answer. First, the whole getting up early thing was for the birds, as I am such a night owl. Second, being mandated to run a certain schedule by a boss when I had been dictating my own hours and schedule for the past 20 years was not going to happen. Was I crazy??? I chuckled at myself and remembered the cliché and added a "not." "The grass is (NOT) always greener on the other side of the fence." I was able to settle at least one question mark and say for sure I was in the right job. I loved my job—it was just super stressful.

Changing jobs wasn't the problem, so what was? I went back to look at my current job. I analyzed what was working and what wasn't. I needed to eliminate some of the stress. Through prayer and counsel with friends, I realized I needed to modify the things in my job that were not working. I made a few changes for the "new" me and my lifestyle, and now I am humming along just fine.

I worked through the same process with all my other questions and determined what was best for my children and myself, looking at each through the lens of God's will for my life.

Finding My Purpose (God's Will)

To know what God's will is for your life is like getting an answer to that million-dollar question.

Let's walk through some practical ways you can find your God-given purpose. Start by asking yourself these questions:

- Do you have a desire?
- Are there any verses that support your desire?
- Are there any verses in Scripture that contradict your desire, or that are in a gray area?

If gray or unclear, ask the following:

- Have I sought the Lord and other wise counsel on this matter?
- Could my own will and desires be causing me to "hear" what I want?
- Is one way **better** than the other?
- Has God given me **clear** direction in this matter?

Let's talk some more about these four points concerning possible gray areas.

Seeking Godly Counsel

I cannot emphasize this enough: pray for guidance in your prayer closet (war room), and then as a precaution against the third point above, reach out to a counselor or wise friend. Ask those confidantes in your inner circle for their opinion. For me, the first 14 months or so, I was living in a brain fog and didn't even know it. It was like I was sitting in a room as the sun began fading away and only realizing how dark it had become when someone switched on the overhead light restoring full visibility. Traumatic breakups affect your reasoning skills. Seek wise counsel.

What Are My Desires Causing Me to Hear?

There are times when our desires will cause us to "hear" what we want and possibly lead us to pour over the Scriptures seeking a verse that supports our thoughts. Be careful of taking one verse and applying it to your life without comparing the Scriptures with the Scriptures. It is very easy to do when we are emotional. It is like we are looking down the barrel of a periscope—little visibility. We need perspective. I once heard someone say, never make a life-changing decision in the midst of a trial; wait 6-12 months before coming to a conclusion. Let your head clear. We don't want to chase one bad decision down with another.

Along this line, I am going to take the time to insert a thought about dating. I know, I know! Some of you are saying, *What?! Are you crazy? Never again!* or *I'm still married!* Others of you may have been separated six months or even longer, and you are getting antsy. You are lonely, and the quickest way to fill that void is to be with someone else. Can I just say, many people have regretted moving into another relationship too quickly. That is where we get the idea of a "rebound" relationship.

I know for me and many others, the first 12-15 months after a separation/divorce, your mind is dealing with the trauma of it all and you are not yourself. You are wounded and need time to heal. Rejection is the #1 emotion you will feel. If you jump in too soon to a new relationship, the wounds go deeper and hurt more, making it even harder to break free of the anger, bitterness, and unforgiveness.

When we are wounded, we tend to attract those with similar wounds. That wound is a common bond. When one or the other begins to heal and move on, people find they do not have anything in common like they thought. Due to their brain being in the "Land of the Fog," as I like to say, it is understandable. So, avoid the rebound issue and avoid dating for at least 12-15 months – minimum! My personal experience and my divorced friends seem to feel at least two years is needed.

Another reason I think it is wise to refrain from dating too early is that our loneliness drives us to God. It forces us to deal with things we didn't really want to because we do not have any distractions; we can deal with them and with godly counsel, in a healthy way.

Once you decide to date, enter the realm SLOWLY and TENTATIVELY. Scientifically, it has been discovered that after you meet that new, wonderful, everything-you've-dreamed-of "hottie" and you begin dating, your body releases chemicals. I read an article that said all those chemicals that are released at different stages take about five months to wear off. The new rule of thumb is, "Don't even think about anything permanent with another person until at least five or six months go by." The old rule of thumb spoken of by wise mommas is to wait a full year. In that amount of time, you can see the character of someone, and it will cull out the mismatched partners. Also, if you are waiting to have sex until marriage, only the good ones will stick around anyway (unless they have someone else, on the side, and that's a lesson for another day).

A Good Way versus the Best Way

Sometimes there may be two paths, and either one is fine, but you want to make sure you pick the best one for you. How are you going to know? That is where asking God to confirm the path is invaluable. I believe this is where most Christians lose it. My hand is raised here, too! When we have two good options, we don't tend to agonize over them, we don't pray about them as much, and we are quick to decide. It is in those moments when daily meetings with the Lord for personal, quiet, prayer time pay off. I am not talking about driving down the road where your mind is distracted kind of prayers but the serious focused, one-on-one consultations. Many times, God would bring me to a verse in the Bible that I "accidentally" turned to. There were times when I didn't get a clear answer, but I had that focused time to talk to my Father about it. I was able to process. Then as I moved through my day, one path became highlighted by a song, a sign on a passing car, or a message from a pastor on the radio. God would show up, but if I was not intent on my conversations with Him, I would have missed those small signs. So, ask God to give clarity on those good versus best options.

Has God Given Clarity

Once you think you have picked the right path, wait for God to confirm your choice, over and over again, until you are positive you made the right one. When I was questioning God about everything in my life, including my church, I used the principle God taught me: "Wait for clarity then seek confirmation."

"They," whoever they are but generally known as the wise ones among us, say confirmation comes at least three times. I don't know if this is set in stone anywhere; I just know it to be a good rule of thumb. Let me give you an example.

I spoke briefly about going to DivorceCare. The DivorceCare classes were not at my church. Another church hosted the class, and I had no intentions of changing churches, and there was absolutely no pressure to do so. Yet, as I was questioning everything, including my church, God kept leading me back to that church, not when I wasn't seeking an answer but only as I was seeking.

In a series of occurrences, in a short amount of time (I think it was three months), God showed me that was the church where I needed to be. It came through prayer and impressions that if I had not been looking for, I would have missed. I bumped into another person who attended that church; I was invited over to one of the leader's houses to play games with the others from the group; I was with a client, and they told me they were invited to go there; and I saw a group of volunteers from that church fixing food at a park for the homeless, along with other highlighted moments.

God was bringing the name of that church before me repeatedly. In the past, the most I would hear about that church or someone who attended it was once or twice per year. See, I had two choices, two churches that were both a good fit for my daughter and me. I was leaning towards the other one, but I wasn't settled about it, so I kept waiting and praying. I sought counsel from two of my mentors. Over the course of the next three months, God directed me to the other church, through prayer and people. I asked for clarity, and God confirmed it was time to leave my previous church. In addition, I sought confirmation from multiple counselors who confirmed where I believed God was leading. "Wait for clarity and seek confirmation."

Unique Revelation

How do you really know what is of God and what's not? I found that God's will and His calling didn't always get revealed in a moment but over time through dreams, signs, and the Word of God. Let me share a couple of times God revealed His will for my life so I could walk in my calling.

My Story

I was wrestling with some of my question marks and asking God for clarity on what He wanted me to do with my life. Here is a clear example of a time God spoke to me through a sign. Back in December 2015, I signed up for a Songwriting clinic which was to be in Indiana in June 2016. It was now June, and I was heading to the conference, excited to see what I could learn and if I had it in me to be a songwriter.

Now, I had never written a song in my life, but I was feeling moved to tell a story, write a song for others to be encouraged. I thought music would be a great outlet for that message. I went to the conference and realized God was giving me a sign. He held up a really big sign. My sassy mind interpreted it as this: "You do not have not one poetic inclination in your entire body! You couldn't rhyme if I paid you." I know I am being facetious, but I was truly horrible. Here is the neat thing about that trip, however. Somehow during those three days, God took my desire to write a song and turned it into a desire to write a devotional workbook which would later turn into a book. There was no song in my future (at least not at that moment).

Sometimes we get on a path thinking we have figured out God's calling. We believe we know exactly what God wants, but while in the discovery mode, we take a rabbit trail or two. That's okay. That's what happened to me and in the process, I learned a lot. Even though I walked away from songwriter school, knowing songwriting wasn't in my wheelhouse, I made several friends.

After the songwriter's clinic ended, I initially thought I would create a workbook, not an actual book because I didn't think I had enough for a book. I presumed a workbook would be perfect. I could tell a little of my story through my journals, give Scriptures, then add some thought-provoking questions with a place for the reader to write out their thoughts. Sort of a guide to healing. God had other plans. He wanted me to write this book, and here it is. Two and a half years in the making (FYI: I took a year off so technically one and a half years. This is for encouragement for other potential authors. Don't give up). As I write this final chapter, I look back on all the pain and can see God leading me through the pain and into a new purpose.

I want to share another incident when God led me into His will. One day, a year after the songwriter's course, I was listening to the radio, and the urge came over me again to write a song. I had all these words stored up ready to burst out. I love music, and it had been a powerful help to me in the last couple of years. I wanted to encourage others just as much as I had been encouraged through music.

When this urge came over me, I was driving down the road. I thought to myself, "Okay, God; I went down this trail before, and we determined writing music was NOT my thing. I know I can't do it by myself, but what if I could find someone to take my feelings, my words, and arrange them into a song that would help others? Who could I call? I have several friends to choose from, and I really don't want to waste anyone's time or pick the wrong person. God, can you give me clarity on who I should call?"

You know those songwriter friends I was telling you about? I kept a few cards in my wallet and would glance at them from time to time, so I remembered their names. One songwriter's name was Margaret, and the other was Krista Melton. As I was talking to God about attempting to co-write a song and who to call, a car drove by. On the back of the car, it had an advertisement for a networking company with the distributors' name. Remember, right at this time I was thinking of both women and debating on calling either Margaret or Krista, and I said, "God, You are going to have to help me decide who to call because I just don't know."

Guess what? This time God answered swiftly and clearly. The distributor's last name was Melton. What are the chances that a car with that last name of the songwriter whose card I had in my wallet, would drive by at just the right time when I was asking for wisdom and clear direction? Isn't that such a God moment? I don't think I have ever seen or known anyone with the last name of Melton. That could have only been orchestrated by an omniscient God who loves me so much. When that happened, I envisioned God leaning down, kissing my forehead, giving me a swift hug as He said, "Love ya, honey." He moved that car down the road at the precise moment to give me a well-defined, tangible sign, a gift to me. Amazing!

I called Krista Melton, and within a couple months we whipped together a song entitled, "Shattered."

I actively searched for God's will in my life, prayed, and waited for signs. He used my desire to lead me down the path of writing this book. And because God loves me, He allowed another desire I had come to fruition. A song was born, and it became like the cherry on top of a very delicious ice cream sundae.

For me, God placed in my heart the idea of writing a book. I felt compelled to journal my thoughts that first year. I had no idea that all my pain and drive to "figure things out" would one day lead to a calling on my life to write a book. Yet, here I am writing the final chapter of my first book. Incredible!

Along this journey, I have been privileged to hear other narratives about how God worked in the lives of other shattered souls. I was blessed to hear and see how God picked up the broken pieces and helped others heal and find their purpose. I asked two of my friends to share a bit of their journey on how God revealed His will and calling for them.

FINDING YOUR PURPOSE

John's Story

"When I hit rock bottom, I was on the threshing floor, alone with no family, few friends, and a failed marriage. As I sank into depression, it was a brother in Christ, Tim, that came alongside me and encouraged me to fight. Tim said the days would get better. I began to believe what he was telling me, although I could not see it. He allowed me to process outwardly all the anger and junk I had inside. When I finished letting it all out, he would speak Scriptures and words of encouragement to me, lifting me up.

What I was not aware of is that God had deposited something inside of me, a competitive spirit, and drive that I would NEVER quit. Not on myself, not on my family, and not on Him. It was a different kind of drive than I had ever experienced. I was fighting to survive, not just to win. I allowed Him into the dark places of my hurt, my pain, and my soul so He could heal me. It was ugly but worth it.

I learned more about relationship (heart knowledge of God) versus religion (head knowledge of God) during this process as Tim walked with me. I saw the Holy Spirit inside him, the peace, kindness, and relationship he had with Jesus, and it inspired me to think of the 'what ifs?' and 'why not me?'"

Along with the Bible and my mentor, Tim, God brought three books into my life that had a profound and lasting effect. They are the following:

Fathered by God *by John Eldredge*
Basic message: Recognizing the stages of being a man (Boyhood, Cowboy, Warrior, Lover, King, and Sage) and how vital it is to be affirmed by our Father, God. Most men are stuck between Cowboy and Warrior.

He-Motions *by TD Jakes*
Basic message: Dealing with emotions in a healthy way. How to be free from expectation, emotional wounds, and step into sonship with God in confidence. Also knowing "we" as men are not alone in this battle and we need each other.

Wild at Heart *by John Eldredge*
Basic message: Dealing with wounds, getting healthy emotionally so a man can effectively fulfill his godly assignment. Recognizing we all have emotional wounds and that Jesus wants to set us free if we only say yes and let Him.

In Wild at Heart, *John Eldredge shares three things a man needs which God provides. They are*

- A battle to fight
- An adventure to live
- A beauty to rescue

These are reflections of the heart of God. God is at the center of life, fulfillment, and purpose.

We are invited to participate in an epic battle God has called us to. He wants us to partner with Him; that is one reason why we were created.

I found my purpose in the Kingdom of God through my pain. If there is not a purpose in the pain, it's just pain. I was restored by letting the Holy Spirit, Jesus, and Father God minister to me, bringing restoration. Each personhood of the Trinity ministered to me in different ways, and there is where I found what God wanted me to do. I realized my identity is in Jesus Christ as a child of God. It was not in a job, in a marriage, or any other worldly possession. I found my purpose: to help other men, as I was helped, through their pain and help them have their hearts awakened to their first love, the love of their Heavenly Father." John Whitfield

John has been such a blessing to me and to a multitude of others. He could have read those books like many others did and just left it at that. He could have chosen not to go to a men's group, and he could have never chosen to lead, but he did. Many lives have been changed because first, he let the Holy Spirit work in his life, cleaning out the anger, bitterness, and unforgiveness. Second, he allowed God to heal his soul and step onto His path of purpose.

Caryn's Story

I was a new Christian when I was going through my breakup. It was a very abusive relationship, and God brought a wise Christian woman into my life. She was able to teach me about God and His will for my life as I walked through that terrible time. I wanted help and was open to hearing God's plan for me. I learned and applied the Scripture she brought to my attention. One, in particular, tells about the Fruit of the Spirit found in Galatians 6:22. It says to look at a man's actions (mine included). I was able to look for these "fruits" or character traits to give me help to determine what was best. Words are cheap, but actions define a person. Understanding the Word of God, then being able to apply it to my life, made the process so much easier.

I didn't know it at the time, but God was showing me His will and calling for my life. He wanted me to learn His Word and to trust Him to guide me through life. I was learning I was to please God over man. For so long in my life, my focus and purpose were wrapped up in what the man in my life wanted with no thought to the One who created me. I had never even realized that God did indeed have a plan and a calling for my life. Now, as a new Christian, I was hearing specific verses that gave me purpose. Those verses gave me wisdom and strength to avoid relationship pitfalls. That knowledge shifted my focus so that God was now the first Person in my life, followed by my son. My calling became

FINDING YOUR PURPOSE

taking that knowledge of who God was and passing it on to my son." Caryn Valle

What I love about Caryn and those with her gift and calling is that they may not be in the public eye on a grandiose platform, as the next testimony below will show, yet she and others like her are quietly touching others' lives behind the scenes. She is an encourager. That is a part of her calling, along with teaching her son God's ways. God is using her to speak into the lives of women around her that need encouragement.

Never, ever, forget that for every outgoing personality or person in the limelight there is ALWAYS a "Caryn" behind the scenes, encouraging and lifting them up when they get down and discouraged.

A great example of the encourager came to me while I was watching the Super Bowl. I noticed several assistants running out during half time with bottles of water to squirt into the mouths of the players. They were also quietly waiting and watching on the sidelines with towels, jackets, and other needed paraphernalia ready in anticipation of the player"s needs. Their job was to keep the players in the game and going strong. The "Caryn's" of the world are like the Team Assistants. The players can't perform at their best without their support. They are very needed. It is a circular relationship—their purposes intertwined, binding together, for the good of the team. In our case as Christians, we are on Christ's Team. GO TEAM!

Esther's Story

One of my favorite historical events is the story of Esther. The retelling of the story opens with a feast held by King Xerxes I in the land of Persia, approximately 475 BC. This is one of the most amazing stories in the Bible revealing God's purpose, as He weaves Himself like a beautiful tapestry through the lives of His children. It is a short book, and I encourage you to read it on your own. When you are finished, I guarantee your heart will be lifted, and you will be praising the Lord for His amazing grace and sovereignty.

The book of Esther is a tale of a young lady whose life took a dramatic turn into a sea of the great unknown. She was a young woman, minding her business in a small town about 150 miles to the north of the Persian Gulf. She had grown up in that town, and it was home. She was known for her beauty, and deductive reasoning would say there were young men pursuing her. Maybe she even had a special someone she daydreamed of spending the rest of her life with. She was full of hopes and dreams, oblivious to the changes about to occur.

One day the whole region was told the King was looking for a new queen. His officers were tasked with gathering up beautiful, young virgins throughout the kingdom. As beautiful as she was, the officers picked her out of the crowd, and she only had a short time to say goodbye to those she loved and gather a few possessions. In the blink of an eye, her life was irrevocably changed. What a helpless feeling.

Sometimes we read these stories and brush right past the feelings of the moment. Take a few minutes and envision yourself at the age of 18-21. Where were you? What were you doing? What would you feel if you were forced to leave everything and everyone you knew to be a possible bride to some unknown man, at best. And at worst, you would be placed in his harem never able to experience life as a cherished wife with a man you loved and to raise your children the way you believed was right?

Think back to the book of Daniel, and imagine being in his shoes. The book of Daniel says he was forcibly taken into slavery, and his captors caused him to be a eunuch. Typically, male servants were placed in charge of the harems of the king, or a chamberlain, or the extremely smart might became advisors to the king and his leaders. In order to ensure they didn't have sex or rape the wives or concubines, they were castrated. Never able to have sex, get married, or have a family – OUCH! The pain and heartache that went along with being forced into a situation they never wanted must have been unbearable.

In both cases, for the men and women who were slaves, they had no say over their bodies. It must have been a depressing and extremely frustrating position to be in. Just as we have been placed into the situation of a separation or a divorce. Many of us never wanted it and never envisioned this kind of life at the age of 18 when we saw things through rose-colored glasses.

Back to the story. Esther's uncle, Mordecai, who raised her after the death of her parents, worked at the palace of Shushan where the King resided along with his harem, slaves, and advisors. When Mordecai found out that she had been brought into the house where the virgins were kept, he daily checked on her. He advised her not to tell anyone she was a Jew, so she kept her lineage a secret. For a year, she went through a purification process, as did all the collected virgins from the entire Persian empire. Once she finished that ritual, she was then presented to the king.

The Bible says she found favor, *"And Esther obtained favour in the sight of all them that looked upon her"* (Esther 2:15b).

And even more! Esther 2:17, *"And the king loved Esther above all the women, and she obtained grace and favour in his sight more than all the virgins; so that he set the royal crown upon her head and made her queen instead of Vashti."*

Esther's life had been forever changed, and she was now stepping into a role she could never have imagined a year or two before. Here she was as queen to one of the largest kingdoms of all times.

Enter the villain of the story by the name of Haman. Haman did not like Mordecai, and he devised an evil plan. As you watch the story unfold, you see a treacherous, scheming plan to kill not only Mordecai but the entire Jewish people in the Persian Empire. That was where Esther came back into the story. She used her position to bring awareness of this travesty to the king. You will have to read the book to see all the amazing twists and turns that happened. I want us to stay focused on God's purpose and plan through the pain.

For Esther, God's purpose in allowing the harsh change ultimately saved an entire group of people from annihilation. That is a sobering thought. We have gone through harsh unwanted changes, and God allowed it. It must make you stop and ask the question, "For what purpose?"

Wrapping it up

As you can see by the above four examples, God worked in everyone's lives uniquely and for a different purpose. God planned for me to write this book; John's purpose is now helping other men find purpose in their pain; Caryn's new purpose was to delve into the Scriptures, to know Jesus more, and pass it on to her son; Esther's purpose was to save a people from annihilation.

> Each and every Christian has a specific calling. No one calling is greater than another—just different.

We need to be willing to surrender our desires to God, fully trusting Him to show us His purpose, in His time. When we walk through pain, we may not always know the reason, but we can be assured God has a plan and a purpose for it.

Out of Pain Comes Purpose

I wonder if Saul, later known as Paul, comprehended that while he was living as a blind man for three days, that his pain and darkness would eventually lead to an entire region hearing about the Messiah. Do you think he understood what his purpose would be from the very beginning? What about when he was beaten or shipwrecked. What about times when his name was dragged into court with false accusations (2 Corinthians 11:22-30)? Do you think he asked, "Is the pain worth it?" And if he had, would anyone fault him? Because he chose to share the message, lives were irrevocably changed for eternity. Paul had it all; fame, fortune, status as the top religious leader of that day. Yet when God radically called him, he simply surrendered.

What about Jonah when he was sitting in a disgusting, mucus-filled, pitch-black stomach of a sea creature? Do you think he ever could've imagined that his message would keep an entire city from being burned to the ground? Destroyed as if they never existed? God used that radical and disgusting situation to get Jonah's attention. He was called, and he surrendered.

Let's remember Ruth of the Old Testament. She wanted to have a baby, but at the time, it had been denied her. Then her husband died, along with her father-in-law and brother-in-law. To top it off with another emotional and hard situation, she chose to leave the only home she knew to travel to a faraway place, leaving behind everyone and everything familiar. Do you think when she purposed in her heart to follow Naomi she could have ever imagined that all her pain would be washed away with hope and love? She was able to have a baby, named Obed, who was the grandfather to King David, and from the line of David came Jesus Christ. God called, she surrendered. Simply miraculous!

Out of pain came purpose for the people in these biblical examples. **I believe with all my heart, out of your pain, there will come purpose, too. It may just not be revealed...yet.** Each one of the people above had to go through a dark time, a time where their souls were surrounded by much pain and darkness. They went through a time when they couldn't see the light at the end of the tunnel.

Paul said, *"For now we see through a glass, darkly; but then face to face: now I know in part; but then shall I know even as also I am known"* (1 Corinthians 13:12a). I'd like to take a little liberty and reword the point Paul was trying to make.

Right now, your life may feel confusing, and the way may not seem clear, but one day that will change. One day the fuzzy image will clear as we come face to face with our Creator, the all-knowing God who loves us. When we yearn to know Him, when we immerse ourselves in who God is, coming face to face with who He is and what He wants for our lives, then our purpose will become crystal clear.

There is a reason you are going through this painful situation. You may not know what it is today, and questions may be going through your mind, as I am sure it did for the people in every biblical example listed. Let God in. Trust in an all-knowing God who wants to pour blessings into your life. Jesus wants to lean down from heaven with a hug and a kiss, giving you a vision for today. Allow the Holy Spirit to work in your heart and mind, stitching up your shattered soul and applying the soothing aloe that only He can give. The healing is there for the taking. Step into your calling today. Surrender to God and allow purpose to come from your pain.

HEALING TOOLS:

Memorize Scripture: *"Thou art worthy, O Lord, to receive glory and honour and power: for thou hast created all things, and for thy pleasure they are and were created"* (Revelation 4:11).

Meditate on the Journal of Psalms: *"Delight thyself also in the LORD; and he shall give thee the desires of thine heart"* (Psalm 37:4).

Praise Often and Daily: Lord, I praise You for giving me the ultimate purpose of bringing glory and honor to Your name. I thank You for creating me just the way I am. You have done exceedingly abundantly more than I could ask or think. I praise You for the gifts You have given me and thank You for bringing purpose out of pain.

Prayer Decree: Heavenly Father, let the desires of my heart come to fruition as I seek Your will and way.

Focused Thought: I will trust that my Heavenly Father knows me better than I know myself and remember that "God's gifts put man's best dreams to shame." Robert Browning

Words of Gratitude

Many people have had input into my life and into this book in numerous ways. I am listing just some, if I forgotten someone, please forgive me now.

First and foremost a huge "thank you" to my children for loving me even when I was unlovable. For supporting me with kind words through texts, emails, and phone calls. For doing the mundane things of life such as moving heavy furniture or fixing an item in the house. Most of all for the gift of being called Mom! I marvel at the uniqueness of each of you. You are amazing and I love you with all my heart. God used you to help pull me through even though you too were going through heartache and pain. From the bottom of my heart – thank you!

To my Father: Dad, thank you for forcing us children to have family devotions, regularly attend church, sacrificially sending us to a Christian school, and for having many Biblical discussions and debates with us, as our father and pastor. If you had conceded on any of the above points, I wouldn't have the knowledge of the Word of God like I do; for that I am very grateful.

To my Mother: Mom, you gave me the love of communication and the art of the wordsmith. I remember how you used to come up with unique words and would over enunciate them. Us kids would mimic you saying it multiple times. In the process of being silly, saying the words with our mouths twisting and opening wide, along with encouragement to read books often, we now have a large vocabulary. You also, along with Dad, truly lived what you taught and read from the Bible. You led by example, taking time out of your day to pray, read the Bible, and journal. You and Dad are authentic Christians, and I am proud to call you mine.

To my siblings and in-laws: Thank you for the support, whenever and however I needed it. A special thanks to my sister, Robin who made herself available whenever I was in crisis mode and needed to cry, rant, yell, or laugh. Sometimes all four outbursts happened in the same conversation and her ability to keep up was stellar.

To my friend Amber Wilson: God knew what He was doing when He put Amber in my life. She has been a wonderful friend and was instrumental in helping me get out of the pit of depression. Thank you so much for all you have done. I could never repay you!

To Pastoral Counselor Larry Lilly: As a speaker and author, I have called Pastor Lilly for advice numerous times. I met him in my early 20's when he came to preach at my father's church. I was impressed with the level of compassion he had for people. Even though the Word of God governed his life he did not use it to beat people over the head. I found myself drawn to his advice in hard times. He has been such a blessing, and I pray many blessings over him and his awesome wife, Joyce.

To an unusually founded friendship Linda Badame - An unexpected yet greatly needed friend that came at just the right time. That friendship amazes me still today. God used Linda to teach me how to listen for that still small voice of the Holy Spirit, how to recognize an attack from the enemy, and how to truly forgive. She was an amazing woman and is greatly missed. Linda, keep dancing on those streets of glory. One day I will see you again.

To my neighbors and good friends Felix and Nydia Adorno: For being my prayer partners, loving on me, and for giving me great advice.

To my clients (turned friends) George and Jeanne Berard who became my adopted parents when mine had to move. God knew that without The Adorno's and Berard's supporting me, I would have had a much harder time. I am ever in your debt.

To all my friends from DivorceCare and Abundant Love: For all the times you let me gush a torrent of feelings, cry tears, and rehash problems then gave me greatly needed advice – I thank you. Having a community of believers to share and pray with has been invaluable to me. You blessed me so much, and I will be forever grateful.

Words Of Gratitude

Editors: Since this is my first book and I really didn't know what I was doing, I called upon three different editors over the course of the past two and a half years. Thank you to Autumn Conley, who helped me hone my craft of using descriptive sentences to make a memorable point. To Heidi Brockbank for helping me see the broader picture. Last by not least, a huge "Thank You" to Melanie Chitwood, without Melanie, this book would not be in your hands. She took, at times, a discombobulated mess and made it into something readable. She coaxed the final version out of me, patiently waiting for me to send an original chapter or an edited version back to her. I can't say thank you loud enough. Melanie, you have been a massive support to me and I appreciate all you have done.

There are a few others I would like to mention. They are those who heard the Holy Spirit say, "Call Valerie, check in on her, pray for her." They would call or text just when I needed a word of encouragement.

Cindy Pelotte
Sherry Kenney
Duska Lovelace
Charmaine Johnson Procopio
Maria King and Kids
Linda Norwalt
Meredith Walton

Caryn Valle

Holly Lyons

Samantha Bibler

John Whitfield

I know I have missed others as the list is long - for those who reached out and gave me a word of encouragement – THANK YOU! God has been so good to place you in my life, on just the right day and in just the right moment. Thank you for praying and encouraging me through a rough season. God bless you all.

Works Cited

Biblesoft's New Exhaustive Strong's Numbers and Concordance with Expanded Greek-Hebrew Dictionary. Biblesoft and International Bible Translators, Inc. 1994.

"Exercise and Depression: Endorphins, Reducing Stress, and More." Webmd.com. https://www.webmd.com/depression/guide/exercise-depression#1.

"Find Help and Healing for the Hurt of Separation and Divorce." http://www.divorcecare.org/. January 31, 2019.

http://www.heavensrainmovie.com/story.php

"How Alcohol Can Lower Inhibitions and Cause You to Make Bad Decisions." Alcohol.org. January 31, 2019, https://www.alcohol.org/effects/inhibitions/.

Sheets, Dutch. "The Power of Hope." *The Story of the Coke Bottle*. Florida: Charisma House 2014

Logan, Jim. "Reclaiming Surrendered Ground." *Jesus is the Glass*. Chicago: Moody Publishers, 2016, Used by permission.

"The Remarkable Story of Norman Cousins – Laugh Off Life." https://sites.google.com/site/laughofflife/page-1

Wikipedia contributors. "Belaying." *Wikipedia, The Free Encyclopedia*. Wikipedia.org. January 2019.

ABOUT THE AUTHOR

Valerie Sullivan is a speaker and author with a heart to help the wounded. She has experienced the devastation of separation and divorce and chooses to help others overcome, as she was helped, so they may live an abundant and free life. She is a mother with a blended family of seven children and is currently a full time Realtor in the greater Greensboro, NC area. To schedule a speaking engagement, leave a comment, or share an inspirational moment go to
www.DeliberatelyDesigned.com

CPSIA information can be obtained
at www.ICGtesting.com
Printed in the USA
JSHW022348160919
1496JS00002B/4